nternational Homosexual Conspiracy

The

International

Homosexual

Conspiracy

Larry-bob Roberts

Manic D Press
San Francisco

Dedicated to Tommy,
my co-conspirator in life

The author gratefully acknowledges Danyol for the cover art;
Betsey Culp and the late Ken Kelley of the *San Francisco Call*,
and Kim Kinakin of *Faggo* (editors at publications in which
some of these pieces previously appeared in slightly different
forms); the hosts, readers, and audiences of open mics where
some of these pieces have been read; subscribers, readers, and
contributors of *Holy Titclamps*; and my friends for their
support, critiques, and advice.

Cover artwork by Danyol (www.danyol.com)

Library of Congress Cataloging-in-Publication Data

Roberts, Larry-bob, 1966-
   The international homosexual conspiracy / Larry-bob Roberts.
      p. cm.
   ISBN 978-1-933149-42-4 (trade pbk. original : alk. paper)
   1.Homosexuality--Humor. 2. United States--Social life and
      customs--Humor. 3. Gay wit and humor. I. Title.
   PN6231.H57R625 2010
   818'.607—dc22
                                        2010032371

Contents

IV. On Indulgence

V. On Popular Culture

VI. On Homosexuality

Nothing should be assumed about anybody's sexuality, including yours

I. On Community

A Society in Dazed Denial

I often have the feeling of wandering through a city of zombies. People have certain pre-programmed destinations and activities, and don't venture beyond them. There is no way I can conceive of that would allow me to enter into the lives of any of these people. What do they ever do to open the way to new social interaction? Do they volunteer, go to social events, attend a church, or participate in local politics? Or is life an endless cycle of work, TV, and inebriation?

The reason for this enquiry is that there is every sign of the world's imminent end... but to keep sane, people must deny this. So they trudge through life with their gazes fixed a short distance ahead, oblivious to the larger landscape.

There's any number of reasons to be fearful. One fear has supplanted the next but the reasons for each fear have not dissipated. Instead, each fear is buried beneath the next like a layer cake with a frosting of denial. Back in the days of Reagan, the fear was nuclear war; added since then have been environmental disaster, disease, unemployment, displacement, and terrorism, among others. Everyone feels helpless to forestall the impending collapse so they keep their heads down and soldier on. Mutiny isn't seen as an option. Such passivity doesn't improve the situation.

On the other hand, the options given for activism are so pathetically ineffective that disillusionment and cynicism are their strongest results. The elation of participation in a huge march gives way to depression when a few hours out on the streets doesn't seem to blunt the drive to destruction that was protested. SUV-burning, lab-bombing, tree-sitting vanguards don't seem to dissuade the purchasers of gas-guzzlers, torturers of monkeys, or choppers of redwood forests.

We've got a society with Stockholm Syndrome; people end up identifying with those who've kidnapped them. We work more for the benefit of the rich than for the common people. We eagerly buy things we don't need, vote for candidates who don't represent our best interests, and pay taxes that make the world a worse place.

Time to clear away the mental debris, try to think without clichés, and see beyond the denial. Time to do our best to stop the runaway train headed down the tracks to destruction.

Creating Community

In our alienated world, we are in search of lost community. We crave connections with other humans. We want to not just be individual bubbles which bump against each other but which do not mingle productively. It's not enough to simply search for the longed-for community. It may not exist yet. Which leads me to this dictum: don't just search for community... create it.

The social frameworks previously created may not contain a place in which the individuals with whom you would wish to relate can find a niche. So it becomes necessary to become an initiator of new social forms. While this may seem to be a difficult task, it is ultimately rewarding.

For example, you may find yourself organizing a spoken word event, a neighborhood organization, a crafts fair, or a discussion group. You'll tailor it to fit a perceived social gap. Hopefully others will also identify with the new niche you've created, and interact in the social space for which you've made room.

Sometimes the form of a social gathering actually prevents interaction. For instance, someone may have organized a dance event that targets a particular type of people (e.g., queer punks). However, because the noise of the event precludes much conversation and no form of icebreaker is provided, the event tends to be cliquey and insular, not allowing for new social interactions to occur.

These same people could be invited to an event like an open reading where they would be able to hear each other speak and then decide to have further interaction with one another. All that would be required to make this a more socially productive experience is a change in venue and activity.

Among the things that I have been involved with that built connections between people are zine publishing, helping to plan queer music and culture festivals, and hosting spoken word open mics. I have also been a participant in other events that have fostered community like open potluck brunches, volunteering to send books to prisoners, and helping out with political campaigns.

Disappointingly, I have persisted in participating in activities that have repeatedly proven to be less than productive. I have still gone to bars at which I knew no more people at the end of the night than at the beginning. I know I should concentrate on attending more socially interactive events but more and more, I am determined to spend my efforts on the more difficult, but ultimately more productive, creation of community-building events.

I encourage people to experiment with initiating these sorts of social outlets. The rewards should be self-evident.

Getting to Know People

What is your calling card? What is the way by which you differentiate yourself when you meet somebody new? How do you introduce yourself and what you do?

My calling card is my zine and website. I can offer an insight into my taste by giving someone a copy of my zine or a card so they can later look up the website where events and my writing are posted. Others can give a CD with their music, or can show a portfolio of their visual art.

In Japan it is supposed to be good manners to keep calling cards in your shirt pocket. This is why: your calling card is like your face. Keeping your cards in your front pants pocket is like keeping your face by your genitals. Keeping your cards in your back pants pocket that is like sitting on your face. You hand your card to someone with both hands, take theirs with both hands, examine it carefully, and then put it by your heart.

How do you introduce yourself? Are there any lines you can say to someone to jump to the place where you have common ground? Whom else do they know? Where else have they seen you? Remind them if they do not remember. Make friends and influence people, and be influenced by them. I don't like to introduce myself by what I do for a living, but rather by what I do for creative activity. I also like to find the same out about other people.

I curate a set of acquaintances, a social circle. A scene. I have published people's writing and art. I list people's events and try to get people to attend them. When I'm at an event I introduce people to one another. Everyone you know now was a stranger to you once. How did you meet them? How did you get to know each other better and more?

If I analyze my phone list and try to recall how I initially met people, the top method turns out to be through zines. In some cases, they're people whom I mailed my zine to and then met in person later, either at events or by arranging to meet. Closely following is the method of being introduced by mutual friends. Next is through electoral politics. There are a few people I have met through the music scene, comedy, work, and volunteering, among other areas. There can be some overlap—the people I've met through friends may also be interested in zines or music, and some of the music scene people I know because of listing their events on my website.

While I have been sexually monogamous, I am socially promiscuous. I have a lot of acquaintances, perhaps not so many close friends. I have a strict definition of friend; I use the term to mean someone to whom I could talk about deeply personal issues, whether my own or theirs. I tend not to make plans to go to events with people, but rather go to the events and talk to people with whom I am acquainted who are there coincidentally. I am not so interested in being famous—i.e., superficially known about by a lot of people whom I have no knowledge of—but rather in knowing a lot of people in a mutual way.

Talking to Strangers

A couple of weeks ago I was on a bus at night in San Francisco, a 1 California to be specific. There was an old guy in one of the front seats talking about baseball with another passenger a few seats away. The man had white hair and some white bristles. He was talking about the difference between then and now, Babe Ruth eating 25 hotdogs and drinking beer before the game. This guy grew up in an orphanage in Ohio and Babe, an orphanage veteran himself, came to visit, pitched a ball, a nun hit a home run and Babe offered to recruit her. This was printed in the paper, a Scripps-Howard paper.

Discussion of the press ensued. The old guy said the job of the press is to report and it's for us to decide if it's true or false.

He made a quip, "Let he who is without a stone commit the first sin." I said, "Nice twist."

The guy asked, "Who was the general who died in 1944 at Normandy?" Turns out it was Theodore Roosevelt's son (though when I looked it up, I found the junior Roosevelt actually died of a heart attack in his tent a month after the famous battle). Roosevelt lost two sons in war; another son had died in an air battle in World War I. The guy asked, "Which other presidents lost sons in battle?" Someone guessed Washington. (Washington had no biological children, though a stepson died of dysentery soon after enlisting. So far as I've found, no other presidential children died in the line of duty.)

The guy asked, "What's the fifth article of the Constitution?" Someone asked Declaration of Independence or Constitution? Constitution. Nobody knew. The fifth article of the Constitution allows for amendment. "People say if you don't like it here, leave, but I say if you don't like it, change it." He pulled out a pocket copy of the Constitution the size of a checkbook. Where do you get one of those? It was his stop and he got off.

After he left, I said to my traveling companion, loud enough to benefit others, "Why should we sit bored on the bus when we could talk to other people? We are all intelligent adults."

Maybe that man sparked something in me because I've been talking to strangers more since that night.

The other night I was walking down Castro Street and there was a punk panhandling outside the burger place by the ice cream store asking for money for a veggie burger. I stopped and reached in my pocket, mentioning that I was a vegetarian also. I was asked if I'd be interested in buying this person a burger and staying around to eat together. I had nothing much better to do, so I said yes.

I was told, "I just got off the train, hopped a boxcar." We ordered our burgers and took a booth to wait for them to be ready. My dining companion showed me pictures of the train-hopping journey, pictures taken inside a boxcar of traveling companions including 12 and 14-year-old runaways who had jumped the train without sufficient blankets or food but were fortunate to meet more experienced travelers.

They had ridden at times in boxcars and at times in Canadian grain cars that have little alcoves in which people can huddle. At one point, the train went through an eight-mile tunnel. People have died from carbon monoxide poisoning in the tunnel but if you know what to do—breathe through a water-soaked cloth and stay warm in your sleeping bag—you'll be fine.

We took our hot burgers to the condiment bar that enables you to load your burger with extras like onions, peppers, and so on. I hadn't eaten here before. It was nice to find a new place to eat.

We started talking more and I revealed my connections in the queer punk scene. It became clear that we had commonalities. Although my comrade had initially told me a female name, he revealed that he identified as a guy. In the Castro, he wasn't sure of acceptance. A lot of people had ignored him panhandling. He had read that there was a study showing gay people were less accepting of trans people than straight people.

He had lived in Philadelphia and worked in an anarchist bookstore I've visited. He silkscreened patches to sell. He had been riding the rails for five years. He'd been at a San Francisco concert I'd attended at Tire Beach during the Dirtybird Queercore Festival in the summer of 1996, seeing the band Behead the Prophet and slamdancing with their singer who had declared the kid, "Queen of the Pit." We had also both been at queer punk band Limpwrist's last Minneapolis show in December of 2002. Someone looking at us, differentiated by his tattoos and my Dockers, might not realize it but we were kindred spirits.

Last night on a Haight Street bus headed downtown there were three punks, two guys and a girl. One of the guys had band patches for Crass sewn to his pants. They asked me what was the best way to get to the Castro. We'd already passed Divisadero. At that point, we might as well continue to Market Street so they could take the underground or a streetcar back there. They had just gotten to town; last place they were at was Santa Cruz. One was from Wisconsin, the other two from Arizona. I gave them some recommendations for what to do in town: Tribe 8 was playing at the Eagle Tavern that night. (They initially didn't know who I was talking about but then one remembered the story of the band's ride on rapper Luke Skyywalker's boat, when they freaked him out with their strap-ons.) I suggested a visit to the huge record store, Amoeba, though they were probably too broke to experience much besides commodity fetish frustration from such a visit. I also mentioned Rainbow Grocery and a certain underground music venue. They got off the bus and we said our goodbyes and headed off in our own directions.

Later that night on the Haight bus home I started talking to what looked like a straight couple I had overheard talking in a non-English language in hushed tones. They were visiting from Amsterdam. I volunteered that I hadn't been there but mentioned my other European visits. After I'd gotten them talking, two other people on the bus joined in who might not have otherwise participated in the conversation. A young woman mentioned that her best friend had recently married a guy from the Netherlands and was living in a small town there. She had visited there but hoped that they would move back to San Francisco. She herself wasn't interested in living in Holland. There was a young guy on the bus too who started talking, not too articulately, about some music venue in Holland—perhaps he hadn't been there himself but knew of bands playing there. He suggested they visit Golden Gate Park. The couple was staying with the woman's sister near the park, actually. As I got off the bus, there was still a flame of conversation going which I'd sparked.

We all have information, and our knowledge can be useful to other people, and their knowledge can be useful or interesting to us. Why sit on the bus alone in a crowd? Start talking to strangers.

What's Your Sign?

For some reason, I'm apparently the only queer in San Francisco who doesn't believe in astrology. Yes, you heard me right—astrology is total bullshit. I'm not sure what is wrong with me. I had my birthday recently and I got all the usual questions. For the record, I'm a Libra, two days from the cusp with whatever goddamn sign comes next. (I know somebody's going to yell out what that is.)

There is no way a bunch of stars millions of miles away which are nowhere near each other are going to affect your life. Did every queer person flunk science class or something?

What if expectant mothers took labor-inducing drugs to make sure their kids had a certain star sign? Can you get star sign reassignment surgery? What if someone were born in outer space? Would it affect their sign if they were in the constellation at the time they were born?

Newspaper astrology is especially ultra-vague. The stuff they say could apply to anyone: it's all selective reading. How come the newspaper doesn't have an astronomy column to tell us when eclipses and meteor showers are?

Most fags in San Francisco would never be caught dead wearing patchouli oil and dreadlocks but they're still all hippie-dippy about astrology. What's my sign? Yield! No. Stop! No wait, my sign is "Do not disturb."

It's not the only superstition queers are into. Tarot cards are popular because people are so passive-aggressive they can't just tell you what they think of you, they need to have the prop of "the cards told me" or astrological incompatibility. "Oh, I'm not breaking up with you because you're not supportive of me being a speed freak and selling all your Madonna CDs for pennies on the dollar at Amoeba—I'm breaking up with you because you're an air sign and I'm a fire sign." Just tell it like it is and don't rely on some phony pseudo-science crutch.

Okay, why don't I just give up and make a bunch of money bilking people? Let me read your palm… "Ah, you have a long gullibility line, a short intelligence line, and your life line is about to be disconnected for lack of payment."

And then there's Chinese Astrology. Like I'm supposed to be Year of the Horse: why should I have anything in common either with a four-legged hoofed animal or someone twelve years younger than me? There are books that combine the two astrology systems so I'm a horse scale I guess. If someone's Year of the Rooster and a Taurus, it must be some sort of cock and bull story.

Astrology fanatics don't care if you don't believe in it. If he finds out your sign, he's going to say, "Oh, that makes perfect sense… you're a skeptic, that's because of your astrological sign." They're all starry-eyed looking through astrological goggles.

The Skeptic Friends Network

"Hello, you've reached the Skeptic Friends Network, this is Kerry, what's your name?"

"Hello, this is Michelle."

"Hi, Michelle, go ahead and tell me what's on your mind."

"Kerry, my mother died recently and I'm wondering if you can get a message through to her?"

"Well, Michelle, you have my deepest sympathy but neither I nor anyone else can communicate with those who are no longer living. Perhaps you could work on resolving your feelings by writing in a journal. Unfortunately, if you had something to say to your mother, she no longer exists."

"But I thought you were a psychic."

"Maybe you meant to dial a different number. Here at the Skeptic Friends Network, we specialize in truth, not lies. Which do you prefer?"

"The truth, naturally, but not all psychics are liars."

"Of course they are. Otherwise they'd be claiming one of the big prizes for proving paranormal phenomena."

"I know how you 900-number people operate. You're just trying to keep me on the line."

"I cannot tell a lie."

—click—

"Hello, Skeptic Friends Network."

"Hi, I got this cookie recipe sent to me over the internet, and I was about to forward it on to a couple hundred of my closest friends but I wanted to check with you first."

"Thank rationality you did. That's an urban legend. When you get an internet chain letter, always do a search on it before sending it out. Even petitions that seem like they're for a good cause often contain email addresses that have been shut down for excessive mail. A good rule of thumb is never forward chain mail of any kind. The cookie recipe does at least make good cookies, though."

"Thanks a bunch, I gotta go, my Doberman is choking on something."

—click—

"Hello, this is Kerry, your skeptic friend."

"Hi Kerry, I was just at a political rally and the politician promised not to raise taxes."

"And did that campaigner also promise not to increase the government's debt?"

"Well, no..."

"And what about basic social services? Any promises on that front?"

"I guess not. Gee thanks, Kerry, you really are skeptical."

—click—

"Hello, Skeptic Friends Network, this is Kerry."

"I was watching this TV commercial and they were showing these toys moving by themselves."

"Wait a minute, how old are you?"

"Six. And a half."

"I can't believe your parents don't have a 900-number block. Anyway, that commercial is misrepresenting what those toys can do. But you already knew that. Good for you for developing your skeptic powers early. Maybe when you're older you too can work for the Skeptic Friends Network. Now I'd better say goodbye before your parents' phone bill gets too big."

—click—

Annoying Personality Disorder

O ye unfortunate victims of annoying personality disorder! I speak of those possessing annoying personalities, not those forced to interact with them. People who seem not to be intentionally evil but helplessly turn others off with their everyday manners or lack thereof. Often they may be mistaken for being stuck-up, egocentric, backstabbing... but they are not actually malicious, simply inept socially.

Is the condition congenital? Hereditary? Its onset is early in life and it is exacerbated by childhood isolation. Other children refuse to play with a strange child and so improper socialization results. All through life, the person remains oblivious to the fact that nearly every person they meet thinks that they're a jerk. There are those who may overlook the quirks, but is leaving the condition uncommented on the best policy? Is there any possible therapy or even cure? It's like halitosis of the personality. Something smells funny but socially it's not supposed to be mention.

I will try to give examples without insulting the victims of the disorder. One variation of the syndrome that I have diagnosed includes the tendency to speak in a whine of a voice, and more often than not the subject of the drone is himself. Otherwise it's gossip about other people. Perhaps the person is a bit self-centered. If I were to dispense some cognitive therapy, it would be to attempt to make the subject of conversation events or objects, rather than the speaker or other people.

There are others who have a variation of the syndrome that involves being extremely high-strung and nervous, speaking rapidly and loudly with an edge of hysteria. The person may be as pleasant as they can, but extended exposure is nonetheless wearing. I am an amateur and cannot prescribe a drug to modify the behavior, but perhaps drinking some chamomile tea, deep breathing, and meditation would help.

There are those who rush to judgment of other people, dismissing easily people whose faults others find tolerable. It's ironic when this behavior is practiced by people who themselves are annoying. Many times shyness is mistaken for arrogance, being busy mistaken for lack of doting solicitude, fatigue mistaken for a snub. Second chances are not given and possibilities of misinterpretation are not entertained. This furthers the social isolation of the individual with annoying personality disorder.

People's self-ignorance of having annoying personality disorder is perhaps a defensive measure. It might be devastating to realize one was helplessly alienating many others whom one has encountered. The hapless sufferer must tell himself that there must be some other reason that people shun them.

There are other annoying behavior traits: lechers, flakes, the dishonest. And then I must wonder if perhaps I'm oblivious to my own condition. Do I also have annoying personality disorder? Is someone able to recognize its presence in their own life? Maybe I'm just suffering from social hypochondria.

Alternatives to Church

Studies show that people who go to church live longer, and it's not just having a delusion that there's a divine being or the positive effects of communion wine on the circulatory system that produces this result, experts say. It's a byproduct of having a regular social outlet and interaction with others as an elderly person (though perhaps the benefits begin accruing at a younger age).

For those of us who do not have a religious or spiritual belief or practice, what alternative social activity can we engage in that will result in similar benefits for us?

One alternative I strongly favor is attendance at open mike events. I attend a spoken word open reading every few weeks. Many take place around San Francisco in different sorts of locations. Sometimes when I arrive early, there's little evidence that the event is going to happen. Other users of the venue are going about their business: in a bar, there might be a crowd of sports fanatics watching the game on TV; at a community health clinic that doubles as a performance venue, some patients may be waiting for their STD results; bookstore customers browse; and at a sex club where one open mike occurs monthly, patrons lounge in towels. But as the time draws near, the reading crowd starts showing up. Someone starts a sign-up list for people who want to participate. People start moving the furniture. Someone tells the pool players not to start another game. Someone puts out a hat for donations to be distributed later among the featured performers.

Some participants read a short piece and don't exhaust their designated time (or their listeners), while others drone on. It's best to leave listeners wanting more, not less. Sometimes the audience dwindles if there are too many readers. However, people who read and leave without listening to others give an impression of selfishness.

What are the disadvantages of this sort of alternative to church? Lack of stability, for one. Who knows how long any particular gathering will continue to exist? Spoken word events come to an end: venues close; the host moves away or gets burned out. There are few official and funded non-profits that sponsor open mikes.

There are other social outlet models, some of which are more church-like. I have heard that in Boston people attend some sort of a secular anarchist church. Maybe they sing old International Workers of the World hymns once chanted by that ancient radical labor union. I hope it's exciting, interactive, and that everyone gets a chance to speak instead of listening to one person preach political sermons. There are also secular free-thinker churches in Texas and elsewhere.

The Radical Faeries around San Francisco have weekly coffee get-togethers on Sunday mornings. They've got non-profit status, they have land up north that's their sanctuary. "Sanctuary" can refer to a church's inner sanctum or to a refuge from the world. I've heard of Radical Faeries forming care circles to take care of aging or sick community members, an alternative family structure.

Churches can be one of society's most age-diverse institutions, and it would be hoped that a similar intergenerational spectrum could be achieved in whatever we choose as different social structures in creating a post-religious participatory culture.

These days I see old radicals on the scene treated in various ways. Some get respect: people listen to their readings and writings, and they're treated with affection. Other more curmudgeonly elders are rejected tacitly or are overtly kicked out of alternative institutions. Some have a small circle of devotees who look after their needs and help them in wrapping up their life's work. Will I be around that long, or will the world collapse in war, disease, and economic disintegration?

Attending open mikes is my form of church. It happens regularly; I see people with whom I have a social relationship. I hear announcements of other events, similar to an old-fashioned church bulletin; I get a chance to express myself when it comes to my turn on the mike. Participating helps me retain my sense of stability, and reminds me that there are people in the world sympathetic to my viewpoint that I can talk to and that will listen and respond. They don't always react well to everything I say, but by and large, we're in tune. There's no God there, but then, there's not really any God in church either.

Appropriating Identity

It is my prerogative as a middle-class, white, U.S.-born male to appropriate the cultural identities of other people. I have the wherewithal to take on the mantle of whatever identity I choose.

Sometimes I do this in a vague way. I simply hope that people mistake me not for someone who's the product of a completely European ancestry but for some sort of mixed race person. Maybe I'm a light-skinned Latino, a Keanu Reeves-like Hapa, a fractional Native American, someone with a drop of African blood, or perhaps a multi-ethnic combination of more than one these. Maybe my straight hair, my prominent nose, the slightly folded corners of my eyes, my pale skin that edges into a yellowish hue, will reveal some un-guessed-at ethnic heritage.

I meet people all the time and don't realize until later that they're actually ethnic. They're secret Latinos or stealthily mixed-race. So, assuming others aren't any more perceptive than I am, maybe people are drawing a similar conclusion about me.

When I'm asked to check a box indicating race or ethnicity on a form, I never take the easy way out by checking "white." I try to select "other" or "multi-ethnic." Because who knows? After all, in some unfathomed recess of my family tree there might be a non-European ancestor lurking. Perhaps someday genetic testing will be available to prove what I'm hoping is true and that I'll be able to escape the trap of being European-American. On the other hand, I'd be scared to find out for sure.

I speak in a unique patois that reveals my origins as someone who went to high school in the inner city (albeit in one of the whitest cities in America) and has never lived in a suburb. I am down with the jive lingo of today's urban street tribe. Some might call me a "wigga." I do so wish people would refrain from player-hating.

I also freely take from sexual identities. I declare myself an honorary lesbian, boldly take the mic at transpeople spoken word nights, and flirt with everyone at bisexual events. I have even been known to pass as straight (it's a fine distinction between that and being closeted, though). I wear t-shirts representing a variety of sexualities.

I hope that I manage to skate the thin line of ambiguity enough to pass as what I am not.

I am a member of the Wannabe tribe. I like having my hands henna'd. I have considered getting cosmetic surgery to look more exotic. My living room looks like the storage vault of an anthropology museum, with all its hand-carved masks and hand-woven wall-hangings. I bedeck myself with exotic jewelry. I pride myself on knowing more about other cultures than people who are full-blooded descendents. I blast the music of many countries on my stereo.

But still, every day I wake up and see a white person staring back at me from the mirror. As much as I try to perceive that familiar face as one that transcends and incorporates all ethnicity, it still looks tragically pale and shallow.

The Art of Homelessness

In San Francisco, across the street from City Hall, there is an art gallery run by the city government's Arts Commission. The gallery doors are not open to the public: the passersby simply look through the windows at the installation inside. The installations change approximately monthly.

On a recent walk by the gallery, I took a look at what was on display. Through one of the windows I could see a life-size sculpture of a soldier crawling on his belly, holding a gun. The sculpture was constructed out of wire and moss, and had ivy growing from it. Underneath the other gallery window, a black man in his 30s was lying fully dressed and wrapped in a blanket.

While homeless people are extremely common in the neighborhood, this might be an artist engaged in a site-specific installation. I walked around the man, eyeing him discreetly, to see if there might be anything about his appearance that would reveal that he was not a bona fide homeless person.

I thought I might talk to him and ask him something but first I tried another approach. I went to the nearby Public Library and called the Arts Commission on the telephone. I worked my way though their voicemail maze but didn't manage to get in direct contact with anybody. So I pulled a dollar out of my wallet, put it in my pocket and headed back to the gallery.

The man was still there but now he was awake and rearranging the blanket around him. I stopped and looked at the other art again. Then, handing over the dollar, I asked the man whether he knew anything, had anything to do with the gallery. He answered that he did not.

I moved on, and walked to the office of the Arts Commission. Nobody was at the reception desk. Various cards, brochures, and grant applications were on the front counter. I picked up a copy of the Cultural Equity Grant proposal guidelines. Various "historically underserved communities" were noted, such as various ethnicities, "Disabled," "LGBT," and women, but poor or homeless people were not among those specifically mentioned.

I rang the bell on the desk but the person who came to the desk was not able to find anything about the artist or artists currently displaying work at the gallery.

I found the questions raised by this accidental art experience more interesting than the experience of many more formal art encounters. Could I do a performance or installation where I would spend some duration outside of a gallery, starting out with a white suit which would gradually become dirty? Would gallery patrons treat me differently than they would treat someone who appeared to be what was expected of an artist in terms of behavior and appearance? Would this be appropriate for me to make such art, or would it be appropriation? It seems that this action would be something that should be done by a homeless (or formerly homeless) person. In the future, should I— by some unlikely misfortune—end up in such a situation, could my homelessness be reinterpreted as art?

Other artists have appropriated the experiences of homeless people in their work. Examples are Lily Tomlin's homeless character in her show, *The Search for Signs of Intelligent Life in the Universe*, and performance artist Penny Arcade's use of panhandling lines in a monologue. There have also been formerly homeless people who have used that experience in their art, such as Lars Eigner's book, *Travels with Lizbeth*.

Making art about homelessness will not lead directly to its solution. Artwork will not result in the creation of housing opportunities, jobs, or treatment options but it stands a better chance than apolitical art of leading people to rethink homelessness.

Meat-Eaters

If there's one thing worse than a self-righteous vegetarian, it's a self-righteous meat-eater. Glorying in their political incorrectness, these arrogant carnivores relish talking about their frequent consumption of veal, pâté de foie gras, and/or fast-food burgers. There are both highbrow and lowbrow meat-eaters but some draw no distinction between filet mignon and carrion.

It seems strange to make such a big deal about a food choice that is simply a default behavior—it's like holding a straight pride parade. How can someone pride themselves on participating in an unnecessary practice that results in cruelty and environmental degradation?

Equally pathetic, though, is the apologetic meat-eater. They sadly admit that they know all about the evils of factory farms, the hormones, prion disease and so on but the most they can manage is to have cut back on red meat. I really don't understand what's so tough about just not eating animals.

Then there's that mysterious creature, the former vegetarian. This person will confess to some past multi-year stretch of the most rigorous macrobiotic diet. Usually the reason cited for abandoning the regimen is a pregnancy or a health crisis or having been deprogrammed from the cult he was in. It's a case of dietary cynicism, an abandonment of once firmly held ideals. Now that I've been a vegetarian for half of my life, it's such an ingrained part of my identity that the chances of becoming a meat-eater are about the same as me becoming heterosexual.

Meat eating seems to be tied to amnesia. Many times I've accepted an invitation from a meat-eater whom I'm sure knows I'm a vegetarian yet when I sit down to eat there's only a side dish that I could eat and even the salad is adulterated with meat. Family gatherings seem to be especially prone to this phenomenon. Maybe I'd be more likely to attend reunions if I came from a vegetarian family.

The first question people seem to ask when they find out someone is a vegetarian is why. But vegetarians have nothing to justify; it should be meat-eaters who should have to explain their dietary quirk.

When I'm annoyed by these characters I just have to remind myself that soon enough they'll be suffering from colon cancer, heart attacks, or sponge-brain. Assuming that I haven't succumbed to anemia or beriberi by that time.

Motorized Vehicles Off the Sidewalk

I am one of those people who still use the sidewalk for its intended purpose: walking. It is ridiculous that I should have to detour out into traffic to avoid cars parked on sidewalks or risk getting run over by motorized scooters. After all, they have a much larger part of city real estate to freely use, namely, the streets. I can't safely walk in the street but sometimes it seems like I can't safely walk on the sidewalks either.

Last week I was walking to an event in the Mission District and from behind me came two young men on motorized vehicles. One was riding one of those ridiculous miniature motorcycles and the other was on one of those scooters with a seat. Neither wore a helmet. I chased after the one on the miniature motorcycle and snagged the hood of his sweatshirt. He screeched to a halt. He got up and asked what my problem was. I held onto him (was I crazy?) and yelled at the yuppies waiting in line at the restaurant, clutching their cellphones, to call the police. The police station was only half a block away and these guys had apparently just driven by it on the sidewalk with their loud vehicles. I said that it is illegal to drive motorized vehicles on the sidewalk. The guy asked me if I was high. (I wasn't, but maybe it looked like I was, considering I was acting crazy and grabbing onto him, and in retrospect that does seem like pretty reckless behavior. But I was feeling self-righteous and invulnerable, and there were plenty of witnesses.)

The guys denied that their motorized vehicles were motorized vehicles. Apparently, they thought they were just toys. I told them they could have hit an old person (they'd just zoomed by a senior housing facility). They said it was none of my business. Eventually they pulled the cords to restart the engines and went zooming up the sidewalk on the other side of the street.

I ran up to the police station and tried to get some attention. Eventually some officers came out but it was too late. There was a Critical Mass bike ride going by and they suggested that the guys could have been part of it but I said that I doubted it. They wandered off, promising emptily to keep an eye out for the guys.

This wasn't the first time that police station had been slow and ineffective at dealing with motorized vehicles on the sidewalk. A few months before about a block away from the station in the other direction, I'd been walking down the sidewalk with a couple of friends when a full-grown adult on a full-sized motorcycle drove it halfway down the block on the sidewalk in order to park and nearly hit my friend Ken. We got in an argument with the guy and eventually he drove off. I got his license plate number and went down to the police station to ask them to take a report. We waited forever at a coffeeshop across the street and finally officers showed up. Ken was able to tell them what had happened. The guy didn't live in San Francisco and it seemed like not much was going to happen.

I have also had another confrontation with a young person on a motor-scooter. I was walking in my neighborhood and a guy on a scooter zoomed by, followed a minute later by a young woman. I blocked her way with my foot and got in a shouting match with her, explaining that she wasn't supposed to be riding it on the sidewalk. She didn't believe me. I called the police station later to verify that I was correct about the law, and I was. I wonder what they tell people at the stores that sell these things. I'm tempted to go to one of them and find out.

Adult bicyclists seem to want to reclaim their childhoods by riding their bikes on the sidewalk. I've even seen people doing this on streets where there is a bike lane only a few feet away on the other side of the curb. They don't seem to realize the safety issues. Recently I saw a bicyclist fly over the hood of a car pulling out of a parking lot driveway. Car drivers, if they looking for anything at all, are looking for people going the speed of pedestrians, not bicyclists whipping down the sidewalk and into streets, alleys, or driveways. And don't get me started on skateboarders (both the homicidal sidewalk riders or the suicidal ones who skate downhill in the street, ignoring stop signs).

Every day there is the routine problem of encountering a car that is parked across a driveway. The owner presumably has a garage, since that is what the driveway leads to but the garage is full of either junk or another superfluous vehicle so the car or monster truck is parked sticking out in the street, blocking traffic. They are appropriating a public space, the sidewalk, as their private parking space.

Partially this is a consequence of San Francisco's unique architecture. Front yards, alleys, and stand-alone garages are rare. Most garages are tuck-unders, in some cases retrofitted into old buildings and accessed using precariously steep driveways.

Then there are the people who don't even make the pretense of parking in a driveway but boldly park with all four wheels firmly on the sidewalk. Just because the sidewalk is as wide as a car doesn't mean that the car should be parked on it. These people make me angry enough to get a sledgehammer and start smashing.

San Francisco passed a law against driving those stupid self-balancing Segway scooters on the sidewalks when the company was busily lobbying governments to legalize their use on sidewalks. The things go faster and weigh more than pedestrians, and are a hazard to the elderly. I'm glad that San Francisco at least made that effort towards keeping sidewalks for pedestrians, even if there are plenty of people who seem to be void of consideration and eager to impinge on pedestrian rights with their motorized vehicles.

Car Harm Reduction

I take a harm reduction approach to car ownership. I'm not yet ready to give up my addiction to cars but I can try to mitigate the damage. Generally, the vehicle stays parked except when it's time for the weekly street cleaning or if it's needed to haul groceries, music equipment, zines from the printer, cats to the vet, or for a drive to the suburbs to shop, or for a road trip to Los Angeles.

The concept of harm reduction comes from public health

concerns for drug users. The idea there is that if you can't get people to immediately stop taking drugs, at least try to get them to lessen their chances of permanent health damage by using clean needles. I'm not addicted to drugs but apparently I'm addicted to the automobile.

I used to have a job up in Marin County to which I carpooled, alternating days of driving with two or three co-workers who also lived in San Francisco. In other words, I had a more hardcore habit than now. Because I often drove to work, it made me more likely to drive at other times. Now I'm so used to taking the bus to work that it's almost automatic not to use the car at night. Fear of not being able to park easily is another motivator for taking the bus. I even sometimes take a cab if it would be a multi-bus journey. I even walk more: may as well get a headstart in case the bus is late.

Sometimes I have relapses, though. I'll just start off on running some little errand and pretty soon I'm joyriding all over town, recklessly parking at meters with minutes ticking down on them. I'll find myself driving and then parking again only blocks from my last stop, a distance I ordinarily would have walked. I've been seduced by the supposed convenience of the automobile which hides its true costs so easily. No car manufacturer has ever installed a device on the dashboard that counts up the money that you're spending as you drive... but then I guess I've never seen a bicycle odometer taht counts the money that you're saving. It's only when I'm finally confronted with a parking ticket that the cost of driving slaps me in the face and puts me on the path to ending my binge and leaving the waste of money parked. The biannual insurance bill or the hassle of a smog-check can also lead me to question the sanity of my approach and urge me on to complete car abstinence.

II. On Communication

Let's Chat

I like to believe that I can stand at the side of the mastodon tar pit of gay male activity and shout advice but I have ended up getting dragged down into it myself. That is my big tragedy. This is a rant against myself. Decrying some compulsive part of me that has become the thing I hate. At the core of all my contempt for gay men and their cultural vacuity is a rage at myself for being part of the problem.

I have wasted countless hours in computer-based chatrooms. I can use the word "wasted" and not feel ambiguous about it. The payback has been very minimal. None of these people has turned into a real-life friend or even a not-so-real-life friend. I have gotten maybe one or two music recommendations.

Spending time in these chatrooms has been time that I could have spent somewhere in the real world, time that is now forever lost.

The typical interaction is so repetitive. There are the same opening gambits: exchange of some basic information that conveys nothing about the person's essential nature. The information is simply about people's physical characteristics. Commonly referred to as "stats," these usually include height, weight, age, location, and—if someone is interested—measurements of genitals.

It's typical to have more than one window of private chat going. Apparently the stimulation from just one window intermittently spitting out responses isn't enough. Sometimes one will be chatting in one window about highbrow topics and in another about the most base sex-talk.

I hate it when I seem to have found someone with whom I have something to chat about and then he never again responds to my emails. Nothing makes me question my self-estimation but I do question how well I have managed to communicate how interesting I really am.

If these people were really all that interesting, I would have met them at a cultural event because I go to so many interesting cultural events. Therefore, they must not be worth knowing because they never go to these events.

The reason chatting can be addictive is that it has a short feedback loop. With something like email, it takes a while to have an exchange. With the instantaneous nature of chatting, you can quickly move from chatting with someone to erotic excitement. It connects with the pleasure center of the brain. You can continue at a medium level of stimulation for hours, stringing along. Time slips away. Pretty soon an afternoon or worse yet—time that should have been spent sleeping—has disappeared from your life, never to be reclaimed.

Some people have managed to meet others through chat with whom they have ended up in real-life relationships but that's akin to some people having won the lottery. It's the exception, rather than the rule.

The term "chat" implies small talk, not deep conversation. It certainly lives down to that description although sometimes things can get philosophical. More often, it's completely banal.

I have given up chat for months at a time, and in a moment of weakness succumbed to revisiting chatrooms. I find many of the same people that were there before, presumably having in the intervening time spent dozens (if not hundreds) of hours in this chatroom. "Is this hell, or am I out of it?," to slightly misquote Marlowe's *Faust*.

I say I don't chat, but I do. It's like people who say they're not into the bar scene but still go to bars and go home disappointed or hook up with someone, only to be disappointed later. In the moment, you may be able to trick yourself into thinking you enjoy chatting but in the end it's a big waste of time. Why don't you use that typing to write something of lasting importance rather than repeating yet again your stats and location?

I just slipped into the second person, saying "you … you," but I mean me. Why am I wasting my own time? How about going to a 12-step meeting or something? I tell myself I can get over this but am I addressing underlying root issues?

I say I'm just going to do it once a month. Even then I end up depressed for days afterwards and not able to attend to my usual schedule.

I don't really need to trade any more badly taken photographs of half-unclothed men with fellow chatters. I've already thrown away megabytes of those in the past and many more gigabytes remain to be downloaded.

I'm warning you, the shit is addictive, and it's better not to start if you haven't already.

Webcam Aesthetics

The framing doesn't say "Cecil Beaton," it says "surveillance camera." But a surveillance camera that the shoplifter/shirt-lifter knows is watching because he set it up himself. The blind eye doesn't know where it's looking. That's why his nude body is halfway out of the picture, his attempted leer cut off by the frame. Too harsh for chiaroscuro, the lighting is all burned highlight or detail-free shadow; no twilit borderland. He, like most amateurs, doesn't know how to act; acting is not the same thing as real feelings but the art of representing those feelings in a way that conveys them to observers. Even though he doesn't know how to communicate, something is communicated. His body accidentally positions itself rather than being posed. He's made the mistake of thinking that "natural" is enough.

He hasn't done any marketing survey, doesn't know what his audience wants. They definitely want him to take his black t-shirt off... which he hasn't done. They'd want his cock hard... which it isn't. Why waste frames on strip-tease? Cut to the money shot. Couldn't he lie back on the bed and show his ass and dick?

His email inbox is filled with such requests but he must ignore them or else pay attention to those who fetishize blurs, underwear, out-of-focus close-ups of blotchy skin. Maybe he's never seen real porn because he never even attempts to ape its conventions.

So much bad attempted porn has been made since the technical innovation of digital photography allowed the creation of images that didn't have to be seen by a photo developer, and the Internet made the distribution of the images easy. Millions of images of ugly nude bodies: badly lit, grainy, out of focus, poorly framed, from unflattering angles, and without pimples airbrushed out. One would think that with access to tools like Photoshop, people would improve their looks but it's never used for subtle purposes, only to graft on the heads of celebrities or larger penises.

It's always surprising when one happens across one of the few images that actually have decent aesthetics. Generally, it's not just a fluke and the person has created a whole suite of such images. For a while, a Scandinavian rubber fetishist posted numerous pictures of himself in homemade get-ups, like a more kinky Leigh Bowery, the images manipulated in the computer like the work of a modern Pierre Molinier. A man in Texas has unusual poses, like an image of himself lying down on a floor with built-in lights. A Midwestern art student posts large and tightly framed sepia-toned photos of himself.

Most images are less artful than an average snapshot. The amputated head—the body without a face—is common. People wish to preserve their anonymity. Sometimes a person posts a website profile with one respectable snapshot, shoulders-up, fully dressed, and there is another photo of what is presumably the same person, nude, and neck-down. The viewer looks at these two photos and tries to integrate them. Is this actually what is claimed: do these two parts make up a whole person? Or is this some sort of fiction, where one or the other picture (or both) does not represent the person purported? An attempt to combine the pictures in Photoshop produces a porn exquisite corpse.

There is also the amputation of the penis. People post photos in which a close-up of a penis, either erect or flaccid, fills most of the frame. Actually, it is the body that is amputated from the penis. The rest of the body is absent. The person is represented only by this part or by an anus or a nipple. Partially this many be because of the low resolution of cameras and the person attempts to get the best image possible by focusing on a close-up. But often the intention and the result is anonymity, and reduction to identification as a sexual organ.

There are bold people who bare all in a frame that includes their face, body, and genitals. Apparently they don't fear being exposed, potentially being seen by friends, lovers, employers, co-workers, parents, priests, or government agents. They are even bold enough to post the pictures publicly... or they have given the pictures in confidence to people who later betrayed that trust by broadcasting the images. Perhaps they are not unafraid of recognition but rather are aroused by the risk and thought of it.

People need to go to remedial art school and take a class in making better images. Don't over or under-expose, frame tightly, take many photos but instead edit selectively, choose interesting poses.

The purpose of these pictures is not aesthetic stimulation, but sexual. People making images of themselves want others to look at their pictures and be aroused and communicate back to the person in the image that they are desirable, perhaps even to the point of wanting sexual consummation. In some cases, the pictures fulfill this aim despite their technical limitations. More often, the images are inadequate to sense whether the details would add up to desire.

Anonymous Cowards

With the advent of the Internet, the ability to speak your mind anonymously has increased. In the past, anonymous speech could take the form of unsigned paper broadsides tacked up or left around for people to pick up but only a few people would see them and someone might see you posting them. The Supreme Court has ruled that such anonymous flyering is a form of protected speech: an anonymous broadside could be posted by someone who would suffer repercussions if their identity was known but there could be community benefit from the information being shared. Now you can post to computer-based message boards and thousands of people can read what you say and nobody will ever know who's saying it.

There's a local political board that I post to sometimes. I've explained who I am on it, and most people know. There are other people who post there under their own names but there are a lot of people who are anonymous.

There's a difference between being anonymous and having a pseudonym. I write under a pseudonym but everyone knows who the person connected with that pseudonym is and many of them know my real name. I'm a little-known public figure. I have used the name "Larry-bob" since the late '80s. I used the name when I first started my zine but included a copyright notice with my legal name. I have used the name on bulletin boards and email lists whenever possible. People identify me with the name. They know that "Larry-bob" and I are identical. So I'm not anonymous, it's my name as much as any other.

There are some people posting on the political board who thought they were being anonymous but their writing provided clues that gave them away and allowed lucky guessers to out their true identities. There are others whose identities have not been revealed. Some of them may not be people who are public figures. If people are public figures, they ought not to speak anonymously because they should stand behind their words rather than manipulating the process without consequences. On the other hand, perhaps a private citizen ought to be able to speak to the process without making their real name known. They may fear reprisal. They may consider themselves whistle-blowers.

People get pissed off when they are outed. Sometimes they quit using the message board. Other times they stay around and post with the same impunity that they did when they thought they were anonymous.

People should be willing to stick to what they write. They should consider their words carefully because it could be around for a long time, especially with the way Internet information is archived. People could do searches on a person's name or email address and find evidence of past statements that could come back to haunt them. If someone knew the right place to look, most of us could be found broadcasting wrongheaded flames or taking ill-advised political positions.

"Anonymous Cowards" is a phrase that I have used as a sort of ad hominem attack on non-registered posters. Ad hominem attacks are one of the no-nos of polite conversation. But it seems foolhardy to engage in discussion with people who can bait or troll without fear of repercussion. Anonymity is the enemy of accountability. I tend to avoid getting into discussions with anonymous posters, particularly ones with whom I don't agree.

I reserve the right to not respond to anonymous cowards, people who spread lies, rumors, and innuendoes without putting their name to the words, people who attack from a safe distance.

With the Office of Homeland Security, who knows how anonymous we actually are? We may all be exposed to the world.

In Momus' song "The Age of Information," he sings, "If you're an interesting person / morally good in your acts/ you have nothing to fear from facts."

The words of anonymous posters can be upsetting, but what can we do? People appeal to the moderator of the board to block people who are acting antisocial. Some boards, including the one I've been discussing, require users to register using a valid email address so the moderator at least has some clues to tell if someone is registering multiple handles or misbehaving in other ways. When warnings are disregarded, a user may be banned from the board.

A positive reason for anonymous posting is an opportunity for people to discuss issues which otherwise might be deemed too embarrassing to discuss, such as issues of health or sexuality.

I wish there were more bulletin boards which allowed individual users to filter posts: to either filter out anonymous posters, or even to specify some registered posters whose posts you wished never to see. It could be confusing to read such a redacted discussion, with gaps and people's responses where those whom you had not blocked were answering those whom you had obliterated from the domain of the read. But it's preferable to have each person set their own preferences of posts to read, rather than to leave it to a moderator.

It's easy to act antisocial when there are no consequences. I prefer to write words I'm not ashamed to have attached to my identity... and my name.

The New Dark Ages

Photographs are a marvelous time machine. It is fascinating to look at camera images taken over a hundred years ago by photographers such as Nadar or Julia Margaret Cameron. They made artistic portraits of their contemporaries, people whose names still resonate in our era: Baudelaire, Bakunin, George Sand, Tennyson, Alice Liddell (the woman for whom, as a child, Lewis Carroll, also a photographer, had created Wonderland).

Yet some who pass before lenses and are frozen by the pressing of a finger may not be captured in such immortality today. A century ago, images were fixed by chemicals then stabilized to last until now. No such certainty exists for the media upon which digital photographs are stored today.

To retrieve the image of an old negative, even if it is cracked or moldy, one need only transmit light through it onto a photosensitive medium or scan directly from a transparency or print. But in a hundred years, will a CD-ROM live up to its acronym of Read Only Memory or will it be unreadable and void of memory?

I have unreadable media only a few years old now in my possession. I also have disks with images I created in a computer art class circa 1990. Some are in the obsolete 5¼ inch floppy disk format. These images I fortunately transferred to more modern media years ago, and copies of those digital files are on my computer. I have other disks that were made on 3½ inch diskettes, a format barely still in use. However, they were created on an Amiga computer, a brand no longer manufactured. I have not yet found any programs on other computer platforms which could read the disks or interpret their stranded magnetic bits into the images I created based on ancient Aztec archaeology. And that's assuming that some magnetic field, moisture, or scratch has not obliterated the information in the time since it was last verified. Even if I could find a hobbyist who still had an Amiga, could the image be converted into a format that could be viewed on another computer? I still have some slides made from images I created at that time, and those are easily viewable with a slide projector or even by just holding the slides up to the light. Light is eternal but microscopic patterns of magnetized material or pits on a compact disc are temporal.

I also have 78 RPM records made three-quarters of a century ago. They can still be played on a record player manufactured three decades ago. I can transfer that information onto a computer and use that to create a CD which I can listen to now. But the original may still be playable long after the CD has glitched into uselessness. While the colors of Super-8 home movies may have faded, they are still viewable, whereas the plastic of some videotapes recorded later has melted into gum.

So many images of the famous exist that some are bound to survive but there are many people who are now children whose baby pictures may disappear. My advice is not to rely completely on the apparent convenience of digital photography and video but to record some images in formats that have proven archival longevity. Otherwise, there may be only a question mark to hold your place in some future family album.

Zines Didn't Change the World

Recently, a college student sent me an email. Her professor had given her a copy of my zine from nearly ten years ago. She asked me a series of questions, and I responded. One of the questions was about what the effect of queer zines on mainstream gay culture had been. I had to answer honestly: almost no effect at all.

I said that a few zine creators like Bruce LaBruce and Donna Dresch had gone on to do work in other areas including film, writing, and music that had more impact than the zines. But generally the mainstream gay world has gone on its way as if the hundreds of queer zines produced over the past fifteen or twenty years had never been pasted together and photocopied.

In fact, zines in general have had little impact on the world. Some zine design ideas have been appropriated and co-opted in commercial design, which is always hungry for concepts. Some stenciled spray-painted form remains but it's just the form severed from the content... hijacked creativity wandering like a zombie, soul sucked out.

On a brighter note, some of the current crop of small press book publishers have roots in the zine world. There are publishing companies that started as photocopy shop projects and evolved into more traditional book publishing. I'm thankful that there are still opportunities to get into print without attaching to a huge corporation with a vestigial publishing arm.

At one time, it seemed like everyone was doing a zine but apparently only a small number of people were doing them. Now everyone has a website, a blog, a social network profile... probably more people than were doing zines. We see how banal people's lives are: they report on their favorite television shows and reproduce the results of automated quizzes they have taken. The world has changed, but us zinesters weren't the ones who changed it. There are some automatic templates that are just filled in and we each become the bubbled-in circles on a machine-readable form. Uniformity results. Creativity in shackles. Color in between the lines.

Zines are more personal than a website because the tools of creating a website limit it to a narrow range of appearance. The various online diary sites add to this problem by providing templates that people barely modify. It's a process of "personalizing" the impersonal. With a zine, it's created from scratch and the personality is inherent to the approach.

Perhaps my zine was less personal because of the desktop publishing software I used. I should have created it from scratch, designed my own fonts, and laid it out with software I'd written myself.

The zine days were one of many last hurrahs for the word printed on paper. Electronic media hasn't yet completely obliterated paper, but printing on pulp will only become less cost-effective and will decrease in the future.

It's not over as of this writing. People are still doing zines. I'm still excited when I get a zine from some far corner of the globe.

I was talking to my friend, Francis, who talked about getting a zine from a person he'd recently met. The zine served as an extension of the person, a way to find out more. Something that can be read in a quiet moment and is likely to be more completely examined, while someone's webpage may simply be opened to the front page and glanced at, never to be explored in depth.

Recently I've been sorting through boxes of zines I packed 10 years ago. I'd reviewed these zines for *Queer Zine Explosion* and *Factsheet Five* in a hurry, written brief summaries, and put them away. I bring them out now, and once again evaluate them. Are they germane to the collection of the GLBT Historical Society of Northern California, where I'm donating them? In some cases, the queer content is negligible. But where else will this material be preserved? Who will be looking at it?

The ideal audience is the same as it was when these zines were produced—a group of people who were very similar to the creators—people who are creative themselves. This time capsule should be opened by the youth of today and tomorrow but it remains largely inaccessible to them in an archive. Friends of mine have started an online queer zine archive at www.QZap.org. But will people bother to download old scanned zines? The youth of today are perhaps lacking in time or inclination to examine even the recent and theoretically resonant past, as more glitzy yet much less relevant media demand attention.

So now the words that were poured out in passion and excitement are lying unread on paper in boxes in a little-visited archive while manufactured excitement which redefines queer as fashion conformity is available on tap from every blaring flat-screen television. Our propaganda may have been more subversive but audience reach of corporate media was infinitely more extensive.

Everyone's a Semiotician

To define: a reader of signs. We all have various skills in the field of recognizing the meaning of symbols encountered. I can look at a tattered wheat-pasted flyer and tell just from the remains of the design who laid it out and what band or action it advertised. That is because I am a flyerer, an attendee of secretive rock shows, ranter of spoken word soirees, and frequenter of comedy haunts. As I tape up my small posters, I note what is already there.

I am not literate in the marks left by graffiti taggers but I am sure a tagger or a cop from the graffiti abatement unit could tell us who left the mark. There are different layers to the urban landscape and I can't read all of them. Some are just texture.

I walk up Polk Street, and down an alley was a sign with hand-painted blue words spelling out "The Floating Corpses." This had apparently been painted elsewhere and then wheat-pasted in this spot. No further information is apparent to the untrained eye but I know that it is the name of a band because I have seen the band perform. I usually find out about their performances from signs on utility poles. Sometimes I do not find out until the date has passed. They do not send email or post to websites, nor do they fax newspapers for listings. They only flyer.

There are other ragged flyers surrounding the name of the band. One looks to be made by an associate of the band, someone who dated someone who was in another band with a member of the Floating Corpses. The sign advertises a benefit. I make a note of it in my appointment book. They won't send me email but I'll add it to my online events list so people will hear about it who won't ever see one of the actual flyers.

Now, the flyerer, left to his own devices, will tend to follow his own interests, namely to put the flyers up in places where they will be the most visible. The perfect formula is to have the flyer in a prominent place where it can be seen but a place where it will not be ripped down before it has had a chance to work its magic (or be covered by another flyer). A pseudo-mathematical formula could be arrived at which maximizes the eyeball-scanning over time. Variables include foot traffic, time wasted by people waiting at traffic lights or restaurant lobbies, quantity of available wall-space, staleness of pre-existing propaganda, correlation between the intended audience of the event and the habituates of the bulletin board location, and so on. Certainly some mental shorthand version of this computation occurs in the mind of the broadside-splatterer.

There are the city's laws about flyering, and then there are the unwritten rules. While it is illegal to post more than one flyer for the same event on a pole, it is also bad manners to hog the limited space.

I know the laws and I pretty much abide by them. I no longer carry a staple gun since it is not legal to post that way. Sometimes I'll even write a posting date on my flyers. Flyers that are oversized take up more room than their fair share. Venues that don't allow flyers for other venues should not expect other venues to allow their flyers.

There are people who flyer for the South of Market live clubs who carry masking tape around their arms, and rip down all the old flyers on a pole and wallpaper it with theirs. They use the excuse that the law states that flyers are to be stuck directly to the pole, not on top of other flyers and sometimes the old flyers violate this rule. It is supposed to be against the law to remove legally posted flyers but I have never heard of this being enforced.

It is better to put a flyer up in a store window since it will stay there longer. Stores that have bulletin boards or allow postings are blessed. I wish there was some way of repaying their community spirit. Perhaps the names of these establishments should be invoked from the stage as though they were unintentional media sponsors of my event.

There are crazy old people whose hobby is ripping down flyers. One man rides a motor scooter around the city wielding a putty-knife, scraping flyers off utility poles. Someone once yelled at me while I was flyering who claimed I was littering. But I was not dropping flyers on the ground: they were affixed to poles with tape. I asked him what he did to participate in the cultural life of San Francisco. He childishly repeated my words in a sing-song voice.

I do tend to take down out-of-date flyers but I don't want to leave a surface too bare. There is refuge in having other flyers up. If yours is the only thing stuck there, someone might rip it down but not too many people are going to bother stripping off a dozen pieces of paper.

There is always a tape dispenser in my backpack. I have a small one now that contains light invisible-style tape rather than the wider packing tape I once used. I'm told I should be a contestant on The Price is Right with my well-stocked purse.

The suburbs are sterile. There is no place for graffiti or flyer-posting or even signs in languages other than English. The same is true of chainstores. Starbuck's never has bulletin boards. There is no place to cry out against the boredom and conformity of the corporate world. Speech is reserved for those who can afford advertising, illuminated signs. All else is mute.

Someday will there be just one bulletin board in the world on which all flyers must be posted, layered deep and instantly covered by new ones. Think of the Democracy Wall at Tiananmen Square.

Because the events that I'm publicizing tend to be aimed at the queer community, I put my postings in bars. I don't know if it works. San Franciscans seem to just go dance or hang out drinking. Sometimes I wonder, while posting at the few bars that allow outside flyers, why they allow me to post considering that hours spent by their customers away from the supply of alcohol and seeing a show elsewhere are money out of their tills.

The first flyer I ever designed was during college. It was for a band some friends of mine were in. I used letters I photocopied out of a Dover clip-art book and glued in place. I posted it around the college campus on the numerous bulletin boards. I made more flyers in college: for bands, for political activities, and for a nascent campus gay group.

These days I design the flyers on a computer. I have designed close to two hundred flyers. With repeating events, oftentimes the new flyers are simply variations on previous flyers, changing only font and art elements. Why redesign from the ground up? On the other hand, sometimes I have trouble telling my designs for different weeks apart. From time to time, I do start over, re-shuffling the elements that must be there—the location, the performers, the time, date, and price. Oh, I almost forgot, a phone number. Nothing like having completed printing a batch of dozens of flyers, only to realize an important piece of information has been omitted.

When I go to the copy shop, I see other flyerers putting together their propaganda. Uninspired designers just recycle others' iconography, hoping to catch some cool cachet secondhand of the image of a rock star who is not performing live at their DJ night. Some people are still using the cut-and-paste method, while others are even more high-tech than me, cranking out dollar-a-page full-color flyers (the door price must be high to recoup that expense). I wait in line at the paper-cutter behind someone who is making postcards for a show. It turns out I know one of the other bands on the bill, and I ask which band he's in. It's a band I haven't seen before, but then, he hasn't seen the band I know. He gives me a card and I add it to my backpack's propaganda nest.

The Disappearance of the Inexplicable

There used to be phenomena for which there was no explanation except the supernatural. Gradually, as science has developed, more and more of the things that used to be inexplicable have found explanations. At this point, there are very few things that are completely inexplicable. We have theories, at least, for most natural phenomena even if they're not fully proven in all cases. There's nothing left to be supernatural.

There's no function for God to perform anymore. He's been laid off.

Not everyone in the world accepts this state of affairs. That's because not everyone receives a modern, scientific, non-religious education. There are still people indoctrinated with claptrap, either by their parents or (worse yet) their schools, and who are never disabused of their misconceptions. Come on, it's a century since Nietzsche declared God dead. His corpse has finished decomposing by now.

Yet had I not been raised by people who believed in religion, would I even need to write this? I still feel disobedient in writing this, as though the ghost of God—if not God himself—were watching me write this. I'm being disrespectful of the dead by writing about God this way. He's not around to defend himself. He can't zap me with lightning. Afterlife threats don't scare me. Are there scientists who believe in individual consciousness after death? Can anyone prove any of this? Does the pope believe it?

Only 150 years ago, everything I can see would be shocking. The cars driving by, the electric lights, the computer I'm typing this on, the words appearing on the screen, the telephone conversation happening downstairs, the neon sign glowing with captured fire. Could God create this, or only the corrupting power of the devil?

If the past century has brought that change, what of the potential fifty years I have remaining on this earth, if something does not destroy me in that time? What changes will occur? Will it all come crashing down and bring a new Dark Age, or will what some call "progress" continue? Will those with the money to speak to the masses continue to keep people in the dark and prevent them from knowing the truth?

Physics, astronomy, chemistry, mathematics, biology, medicine, psychology: these have laid bare the foundations of the cosmic universe and the underpinnings of the body and mind. The explanations provided are so much more satisfactory than those given by religion, astrology, and mysticism.

Yet some people persist in these beliefs. Perhaps science does not comfort them. They have nostalgia for the time when mysteries were explained by other means. They wish for a world where there are external forces that are not just laws of physics.

I don't miss the phantom world. I can take existence as it is, governed by physical laws which may not all yet be known, some corners still unexplained, still inexplicable.

Seeking Enlightenment

Only an unenlightened person would seek enlightenment. Gee, that's almost a koan.

It's ironic that when someone who seeks to be enlightened is supposedly seeking to lose their sense that there is a difference between their self and the universe, they are actually focusing on themselves rather than on the suffering in the world. Seeking enlightenment is selfish.

Some yuppie off on a spiritual quest in India trying to get enlightened is not doing anything to lessen the suffering of the people surrounding him. The expensive hotel room he stays in may trickle down some minuscule amount to the person who cleans the room but mostly it is enriching some hotel owner.

On the other hand, I, who am not a spiritual seeker, am also not doing much to alleviate the suffering of the world. Welcome to my hypocrisy.

Where is the person or book pointing the way to alleviating the suffering of the world? Where is spiritual or political enlightenment or improvement of physical needs for the poor of this block, this city, this country, or any other?

There are all the Marxist and other revolutionary movements which promise a pie in the sky utopia on this earth. I don't have faith that they will achieve that end any more than such movements did at other times of greater foment than now. If there wasn't a political revolution at the height of the demographic curve when the baby boom was young and radical, it's not going to happen now, when the corporate grip on politics has tightened further and capitalist propaganda is more effective than ever.

I try to take smaller steps, admittedly short of revolution, but which I hope make life better. The thing that I seem to be spending time on now is opening the channels of communication between individuals through spoken word and publishing. Sometimes I seem to just be preaching to a converted choir. Maybe I should be working more on tutoring kids, getting out of my big liberal city rut, and otherwise seeking fresh ground.

I wonder if a world where the voices which support unjust power speak loudest can be reformed. It seems like a greater truth should cause a resonance in people when they hear it. One by one we recommend to each other the books which expose the centuries of lies and reveal the brutality with which the world is ruled.

Maybe only an unenlightened person would seek enlightenment. But being a non-seeker doesn't imply that you're already enlightened. It could just mean you're a spiritual couch potato uninterested in making an improvement.

III. On Writing

Middle Class Writer

It sucks being a middle class writer. If I were some rich fucker, I would have a passkey to the privileged world of publication in snooty East Coast literary magazines. I could write about parental neglect suffered when my rich parents left me in the care of a nanny. I'd have no worries about working. I could write constantly. I could travel to Italy and write about my experiences abroad.

Or if I was working class I could write about my tough childhood... the poverty, the hunger. I could write about parental neglect when my mother left me so she could work for rich people as a nanny. I would have an interesting factory job with crusty working class co-workers. Class consciousness would be a source of political relevancy.

Nobody wants to read about the vanilla suburban childhood of the middle class (though I take pains to make clear that I've never lived in a suburb myself). Upper class writers can write of their hallowed prep school days or Ivy League reveries but public high school and bland Midwestern Lutheran liberal arts colleges are dull.

And forget your middle class office job as source of material for writing. That's completely pointless. The bureaucracies of academia, business, and government are designed to provide job security for socially unnecessary office workers, which is the reason that office politics are so petty and offer a paucity of symbolic grist for literary mills.

Think of the classics written about the poor: books by Dickens, Steinbeck, Zora Neale Hurston. Even more of the canon is about the subject of the rich. The most that the middle class can be is the object of satire such as Sinclair Lewis's *Babbitt*, though the rich can also be satirized. Satirizing the poor is simply tasteless, kicking the already oppressed instead of the pricks.

I could write about secondhand experience: my mother's of growing up in a large family with a father who sold bibles; my father's of growing up with a father who worked in a dynamite factory; my brother's of quitting college to move to Alabama and work in steel mills and airplane plants. But that's not really fair to claim the benefits of working class life without experiencing the hardships.

Pity me, you rich bastards and poor noble workers! How can I rise above my intrinsic blandness? If I write what I know, my audience will fall asleep. I have to fake a blue collar consciousness or be a bounder with upper class pretensions. Otherwise, I'm only a prose Dilbert. That's why I applaud the shrinking of the middle class: a growing underclass and a more lofty elite can only advance the cause of art.

A General Audience

I want to write for a general audience. Well, actually, I want to write about the stuff I want to write about, but I want a general audience to read it.

I am a homosexual gentleman. For quite some time, it seems that I have been narrowcasting my media towards the senses of fellow homosexuals—though not necessarily ones who are biological males such as myself. It seems my most receptive audience has been punk dykes and tranny boys who are the most supportive of spoken word rants of the sort that I expound. Traditional danceclub-going gay men are not aware of my work, apparently. Their loss.

But I would like my words to also be received by heterosexual people. Perhaps I was incarnated in my corporeal form with a calling to minister to the queer people. But why shouldn't straights also benefit from the blessings of my wisdom?

There are certain other homosexual writers who have achieved some sort of crossover audience. Their writings, which may or may not be primarily concerned with fact or fiction on homosexual topics, are read by more than just a coterie of heterosexual readers. One sees apparently straight people reading these books on the bus. There are many other homosexual writers, some of whom are very talented, who don't seem to have heterosexual readers. In some cases, it may be simply a result of marketing. These people find print through publishers or imprints that attempt only to sell to homosexuals. The books are reviewed primarily in homosexual publications. Straight people never entertain a thought that they might browse through the gay fiction section of their favorite bookstore for some light reading.

Liberal white people feel that part of their duty as consumers of art is to absorb a certain nutritional allowance of works by people with different perspectives than their own. This generally translates to reading the work of a few select writers of color and feminists, but there are many who are as neglected by this audience as the aforementioned homosexual lady and gentlemen writers. My idea of a general audience is wider than just white liberals, however.

I recently had the opportunity to write a column for a publication with a general audience. It was interesting to try to write for an audience about whom I could assume little. It could be that they knew nothing about my topics, or it could be that they knew quite a bit and would resent being talked down to. So I had to make sure to explain context without condescension. I didn't write exclusively about topics related to homosexuality but would occasionally touch tangentially when appropriate. The responses received were gratifying. I would like to continue to receive that sort of attention. I don't want to leave the representation of homosexuality to the corporate media versions. For the last few issues of my zine, *Holy Titclamps*, I removed the specifically gay label. Homosexual readers will always manage to find me, but I want to avoid self-ghettoization.

Failed Article Pitches

An idea was pitched to a national gay glossy magazine. I wanted to write an article about the spoken word scene, with highlights of venues around the United States and England. I got a note saying that my contact at the magazine had been unable to interest other people… because it didn't have a celebrity angle. Several months before, I'd naively tried pitching an article about gay coffeehouses to a porn-oriented gay magazine. My idea was rejected, with the explanation that stories for the magazine needed to have a sex angle.

Both of my ideas could be presumed to be a little dull but I have the compositional skills to make them interesting. There are angles of these stories that satisfy the required specifications in a mild way. There are people whom I would consider celebrities, queers involved in the spoken word scene, like Lynn Breedlove of Tribe 8, or if you require the validation of cable television, Staceyann Chin of HBO's *Def*

Poetry Jam.

Isn't going to a coffeeshop a way to meet like-minded folks who could be future sex friends? In fact, isn't that the whole point of the article being about "gay" coffeeshops? Does the payoff have to be so immediate? Does it have to be a coffeeshop with gyrating baristas in g-strings for it to be relevant to gay people?

The need for celebrities—and mainstream ones, at that—is troublesome. Gay glossies regularly feature straight celebs on the covers while the sex mags feature "straight" models. We can't even get pictured in our own magazines. Does gay culture as a whole suffer from poor self-esteem?

Never forget that the point of glossy magazines is to deliver readers' eyeballs to advertisers. Preferably those eyeballs should be attached to people with plenty of money to spend. The objective quality of the content is irrelevant. People who are enticed to buy magazines because of the celebrities on the covers have passed a test: they are attracted to mass-marketed concoctions. Those of us for whom the celebrity is meaningless are irrelevant to the market. A gay man has been redefined to mean someone who has been conditioned to buy products related to particular celebrities. If you have not properly responded to the conditioning, you're now officially outside of the demographic.

Sex sells, but who's buying? Sex can be had for free. Sexual fantasies can be created by looking at people on the street and using your imagination. But there is money to be made from convincing people that they need to buy fantasies created by photographers and air-brushers. Is it only residual guilt that causes people to buy a magazine that might contain actual articles in addition to the Photoshopped photos, questionably "true"stories, and laughable fiction? Are the articles a way of justifying the purchase of the nude photographs? Or is it the publisher's way of justifying spending one's life editing a porn magazine?

Sex and celebrities: two things that can sell a magazine and provide a bed for advertising. Both are retreating fantasies in which the reader never directly participates. Both the stars and the hot bodies are far away in mythic Hollywood, never to be met by the person viewing their artificial photographs. My idea pitches about experiences people could directly engage in are deemed irrelevant. Is it any wonder that I've been relegated to being a self-published crank?

Something Meaningful

Someone's going to say that I don't write about important stuff. I waste my energy on trivial topics that don't make much of a difference. I should be using my talents to shape opinions on world-shaking topics. I should be writing speeches about war and peace, not about music and clothes.

What is considered meaningful has a very personal determination. The things that spark an emotional response have meaning. If something makes me angry, even if it is only a pique at some vexing trivial thing, it is something that has brought my attention to a sharp point of focus; it is enough to justify resolution of my feelings on the matter through writing. Perhaps that tantrum should be discarded rather than sharing my neurosis with the world. That sort of judgment could be accepted from an editor whom I trusted.

Or the emotion demanding response might be enthusiasm. It could be enthusiasm for a song that melodically and lyrically stirs something within me. It could be the overwhelming urge to share information about an obscure writer or eccentric figure. To block the expression of enthusiasm over worries that it wasn't important enough would be thwarting one among my most basic joys.

I don't usually have unique first-hand knowledge of information about the world's most pressing problems. Sometimes, if I'm lucky, I can create a synergy between the items of information that I do have, expressing a new vista on larger concerns. In the meantime, I keep my skills in sardonically overwrought prose honed by observing more quotidian topics.

It's a false dichotomy to say that writing about trivial things means one can't also write about important topics. There is enough time and paper to do both.

Ghostwriter to the World

I'm ghostwriting the world's autobiography. From a lengthy series of conversations, I learned its cadences and have put down in writing the way the world would write if it wasn't illiterate. So now I am, I suppose, guilty of a kind of plagiarism; I stole the earth's secret story and left it uncompensated.

There were secrets meant only for my ears that I now have broadcast to all who can hear. There were sights meant only for my eyes which I have captured and relayed in imperfect impressions. The earth might say I'm a traitor but I am only honest in revealing truths, not a distorter, not a dissembler. My own perspective is included but there are billions of flavors of objectivity and people are free to select the one that most closely matches their own taste.

There is no way to condense the narrative and also make it complete. This is only a selected subset of the autobiography of the world as told to me. This is an abridgment of a tale that will never be published in full. The world knows all but tells only some of it.

The world is not a subject exclusive to me. Those with ears to listen and eyes to see can attempt their own account. Plagiarizing my effort would be pointless since there's no sense in listening to an echo instead of the original note. Out of the cacophony any melody may be extracted. It's a matter of selective hearing.

People have been trying this feat of inspired writing for all time. All writing is automatic writing; we all operate Ouija boards or scribble blindly on small, wood-framed chalkboards. Twigs fall from trees, they can be interpreted using the I Ching. Who needs tools of augury when a pen and pencil will do the trick? All writing springs from the dark unknown. The conscious mind is only partially in control; there is a stream gushing forth that supplies the words though sometimes the trickle seems blocked. But the writer complaining of writer's block still has a voice to complain and has no trouble in finding the words to do so.

The world needs to be cut into small pieces. The whole is too much to absorb. So people like me slice it fine and present a sampler's menu, enough to savor the flavors without gorging on all there is. Nobody can swallow the earth; we can only taste.

IV. On Indulgence

My Name is Larry and I'm a Teetotaler

Hello. My name is Larry and I'm a teetotaler. Yes. I don't drink. I've been this way for a long time—all my life, in fact—and it's time I did something.

I've thought about trying to be moderate. There's the danger of not dealing with the underlying issues though... becoming a wet teetotaler. By the time someone has reached their forties they should deal with their chemical issues. And it's not just alcohol with me: I also don't use pot, cigarettes, smack, speed, ecstasy, acid, or even coffee. As you can see, the problem is deep. Some might diagnose me as having control issues.

Sometimes I see homeless people on the street. I can see that, like me, they're non-drinkers. It seems like if you've hit rock bottom like that, you would examine your situation, and realize that being a non-drinker was not helping your situation, and at least make a start on resolving that issue. But no doubt the pressures of daily life preclude such a realization. I know that I can't go around judging others... I have to work on my own issues.

I know there are groups out there that can help me but I've always thought I could just deal with it on my own. I'm beginning to come to the conclusion that I need to give in and join a group.

There are all the people I need to make restitution to: all the people whose feelings I hurt by waving aside proffered pot pipes, the dudes I declined to get drunk with. The sooner I begin making amends, the better.

I can't really blame my parents. They are normal, moderate social drinkers. I suppose I could blame society: all those ads for non-alcoholic beverages like milk and soda on billboards I see every day. And there is the pressure from the entertainment industry: all those Minor Threat records I listened to when I was young and impressionable.

I know I just need to sit down with a drink—take a good sip—and realize today is the first day of the rest of my life.

Emptiness Inside

There is a longing in the heart of every human, but he is not quite sure for what he pines. In a blind quest to fulfill that ache, he attempts to numb it in many ways: with chemicals, with sex, with spending sprees, with overeating. This void is endemic to contemporary times and perhaps to all times since the prehistoric Eden of hunter-gatherers.

There is a fantasy of what will meet those needs but oftentimes even if that fantasy was achieved, the ennui would remain. The fantasy may be of being the centerpiece of a penetration orgy, of being drugged numb or in ecstasy, of purchasing some rare bauble, of eating to (and beyond) satiety. But still in that physical fullness dwells psychic emptiness.

I prescribe no spiritual panacea, nor predict happiness from temperance, monogamy, thrift, and dietary austerity. For surely I have practiced these to greater or lesser success, yet often find myself spinning fantasies of the mirage of fulfillment that nonetheless retreats.

Buddhism suggests that we try to become empty rather than full, to achieve bliss through the freedom from desire. Other religious and cultural beliefs suggest giving away possessions. But I mistrust this emptiness. We cannot always be in meditation that avoids thought. We are not beings of pure denial; we have needs and these desires are their manifestation. Perhaps this is the false insight of an unenlightened being, but then most beings are—at present—far from transcendent. Spiritual ascendancy over worldly want is, for many, a false hope. The burdens will remain. The trance yet another temporary transport like drugs, sex, consumption, and food.

When I come into real life contact with an indulger, I am reluctant to condemn directly. I may question Socratically whether the person's behavior is consistent with their beliefs about reality. Why do you feel the need to drink? How do you feel after having participated in an orgy? Is your behavior chosen with true free will or is it an inexplicable compulsion? Yet when the person responds to these questions with shame, is this in any way a step towards a happier life?

One of my own fantasies is that it is possible to have physical love with every attractive (by my own unusual definition) man I meet without provoking jealousy. But the existence of jealousy, the lack of mutual desire, and the need to not lose the love I already have is what makes this an unattainable fantasy. Not all fantasies are rational. I try to avoid walking after mirages, preferring to remain in a proven oasis.

I have created a mental equation between big male arms and my own potential feeling of physical safety. I imagine myself in an embrace, two hearts separated only by a little flesh and bone, a fullness that surrounds. I fantasize that I could successfully approach any man about whom I have this fantasy and ask him for a hug and he would bestow it. I imagine at any moment an instant bond of comradely love, and this ideal is proof of its own non-existence.

Daily we are confronted by reality as it exists, and that prospect numbs and saddens. Our hopes constantly dashed, left stranded in an inhospitable environment and unable to change. But perhaps it is our lack of acceptance of what clearly exists that enables us to continue from day to day.

A photograph and a few words of description can be the foundation of a fantasy that love might be found through the Internet. We rely on another person's self-description which may itself be false, either intentionally or through lack of self-insight. Fairytales have programmed us for romance. We hope that we will find another person whose quest for fulfillment will not be incompatible with our own.

The worst horror is to discover incompatibility too late, to find that a person whom one assumed wanted only one's own happiness instead was solely interested in his or her own. And that the other person's pursuit of their desires had left one in a damaged state of health, finances, possessions, or mental well-being. The resulting devastation makes one reluctant to try again to find love.

Ultimately we must come to an acceptance of the ongoing existence of the feeling of emptiness. Just as daily hunger leads us to efforts that enable us to eat, this spiritual hunger compels us to seek. In parallel, as it is best to consume healthy food despite the panoply of edible garbage available, we should seek to fill our spiritual gullets with fare of the highest and most balanced quality.

Party and Play

The abbreviation "PNP" has been appearing in online personal ads recently. It's short for the phrase "Party and Play." It sounds innocent enough: who doesn't like a little birthday cake and a round of hopscotch? But what the people using the term actually mean by "party" is doing drugs—methamphetamines particularly—and by "play" they mean having sex.

There is also an inquiry ("Do you party?") to ask whether someone does crystal. It seems an ironic term for use of a drug with end consequences that are anything but a party. It makes using crystal sound harmless, just playing around. So much of the terminology seems light: compare "tweaker" with "junkie." Or the campy nicknaming of the drug: "Tina," short for "Christina."

But this drug has led people to lose jobs, friends, and living spaces, and had consequences on future life through disruption of education and advancement.

There is not such a thing as casual crystal use. The drug is too addictive. There's no point in experimenting with that drug. The experiment has been performed enough times, and the result is always the same: a descending spiral of lost time, money, friends, and potential.

When so many people have already become messes using the stuff, why bother trying to see if you're perhaps the one in a thousand who can just use the stuff a few times without wrecking your life? Yet despite warnings, every day there is still someone who uses the crap for the first time.

The term "party" at one time perhaps referred to just drinking or toking, but in San Francisco in the early 21st century, the context has shifted to refer to crystal. It's a slippery slope of drug terminology. There is no lexographer making sure that the meaning of slang terms stays constant.

The innocent term "play" packages what may be potentially disease-transmitting sex. Under the influence of crystal, apparently a feeling of invulnerability takes over and previously set limits about using caution when having sex are thrown aside.

Online message boards frequently include queries from people confused by terms like "party favors" who wonder what people are actually asking for. The legal prohibition of drugs leads to the need for ambiguous street terms, though that is not an argument for universal legalization, which I am no longer certain is a good idea. Even if the substance was legalized, having dangerously flammable drug manufacturing labs should still be prohibited.

Hysteria over relatively mild substances like marijuana has contributed to people ignoring warnings about hard drugs. In this case, the hysteria is warranted.

There are those who are convinced that a "Just Say No" approach doesn't work and that harm reduction is important. But the two messages are not incompatible. We can say that doing the stuff is a bad idea, and offer harm reduction at the same time.

V. On Popular Culture

The Unknown Homo

Lesbians in San Francisco are more likely to know who I am than gay men are. My main public venue is K'vetsh, a punk dyke spoken word open mike. These are my people. In the Castro, I'm beneath notice. Who are gay men aware of? Porn stars, dance divas, DJs, drag queens, musical theatre. If your name is Jeff Stryker or Cher or Keoki or Sarah Brightman, gay men know who you are. The route of being a porn star is not open to me, nor is becoming a well-known porn director (who happens to be a drag queen) like Chi Chi LaRue. I am not about to be a dance music diva, although I might be able to come up with language sassy enough to write lyrics for a bitch track. My tolerance for house music is far too low to become a well-known circuit party DJ booth draw. A series of repetitive beats is not part of a music I want to be part of perpetuating. I'm not heading for Broadway or the East End anytime soon. I like music and theatre, but the combination is something I'm no expert in.

None of these options are available to me. I'm also not willing to commit a notorious crime, sleep with enough people so everyone knows my body (if not my name), or run for political office. I cringe at the thought of becoming a drag queen in desperation of attention. I shy from the idea of donning a leather harness to host contests. I fear nothing more than cruise ships full of gay men.

I want to have influence on a culture that is fully off on the wrong track. Really I should know that those who are already adults are lost causes. Best to just try to find those who are already subcultural and band them together. The fags who spent the '80s listening to Hüsker Dü and the Minutemen, like me. They should all be aware. I'm pretty sure a fair number of them are somewhat connected to what I'm involved with already. I've been doing my thing for long enough but irregularly enough that I'm just a germ in the back of their minds, not a full-time obsession. There is some sort of underground queer pantheon— among its lights are Vaginal Davis, G.B. Jones, Lynn Breedlove, Bruce LaBruce, Justin Bond, Michelle Tea, Dennis Cooper, Donna Dresch. Not as overexposed as the platinum-wigged disco divas and porn stars whose images have been implanted in replacement of the brains of the gay circuit crowd. You have to take several turns off Broadway side streets to get there.

I refuse to admit that I have been rejected by mainstream gay culture. Instead I prefer to say that I have done the rejecting. Gay culture is just too vain and stuck up to realize that it's been shunned.

Fags... Go Figure

I'm jealous of the punk dykes. Reading their slam poetry in pitted-out t-shirts, strutting with leather pants and strap-on on-stage, not conflicted about monogamy, unselfconsciously evil. Not eager to become lipstick lesbians but, in some cases, dirty femme angels. Dangerous in tattooed rage, flamingly butch.

And they have community spaces, bars, coffeeshops. Sisterhood is powerful. Brotherhood is in danger of becoming just another boy's club and reinventing the patriarchy. Lesbians have feminism but what do us sissy boys have to be the theory behind our practice?

We have to be shy because otherwise it might mean we're interested and horny and sexual and therefore no different than those men who died, society tells us, because they were evil. And we assume if a guy's not talking to us, it's not because he's shy but because he's stuck-up. Well, it takes two to not talk.

When I go to see the bands, go to see the poetry slams, there are more dykes than boys. Dykes making out or slamming violent in the pit, while the boys stay in their clique or hang out as shy or creepy wallflowers. But there are always more dykes than fags.

That punk dyke scene isn't just a recreation of the straight boy punk scene. It's a re-invention, re-interpretation. Got some new goddesses dug out of the trash bin. Straight boys don't get it, pan the records without hearing the music. Those boys' punk is Rush Limbaugh with a mohawk. Why even bother if it's no different than what you claim to rebel against?

Given the example of dyke punk subversion, perhaps the punk sissy wears a dress instead of forming yet another slam-pit, finding inspiration in a more truly defiant rebellion.

Maybe it's just San Francisco, but when I go to a radical queer gathering in New York, once again: tons of punk dykes. It's great but where are the fags, and what are they doing instead of this kind of fun? Why can't I be a shiny happy disco boy drugged out of my mind, with Ecstasy to give me ecstasy? Shouldn't I be happy that some barrier keeps out the boring ones, weeds out the pretty ones, since I (for one) don't crave pretty boys?

There's that magazine that might be for youth and it might be for dirty old men. It's about big pants and cute boys... the ugly ones and icky girls can just commit suicide. And who knows if the magazine brainwashes the boys or if that's really how boys think? Malls are malls, whether they're lined with Gaps or with rainbow flags and bootleg house compilations. Maybe their minds were rotted by Super Sugar Crisp before they ever heard of freedom rings.

Maybe that young gay boy thinks punk means he won't have a money-making job and decides to assimilate instead, since gay boy yuppies are visible success stories everywhere, while baby dyke thinks she'll never make it to even the first rung of the corporate ladder without a role model and therefore wears a mohawk. I have a corporate computer job and still do non-mainstream zine and music stuff, and I know punk computer-savvy dykes who do, too.

I don't even think of myself as "punk" anymore, if punk just means wearing jackets with band names older than their wearers. What's the difference between that and the wannabe Deadheads on Haight Street? What was once about breaking rules is now about following them. I don't like limits, and "because that song isn't punk" is a limit.

Consuming is the same whether it's the Subhumans or Madonna. Giving life meaning is about continuing creation, baked fresh like bread, doing it yourself despite the advertising. And you don't have to wear leather or spikes to do it yourself, you can be square and still be creative. There's also the pitfall of boutique hair dye: guys who look the look but have never created anything, or have created for the wrong reasons... to be popular, to reinforce their clique, to build a career.

So maybe I like better hanging out at the margins of the punk dyke scene than I would in any potential all-fag scene.

Modern Rock Divas

It's a Friday night, and a 20-something gay guy named Bruce has just gotten lucky (or so he thinks). The guy he danced with at the gay bar invited him home. While his host is showering off the club sweat, Bruce looks around the tastefully decorated apartment. Everything seems relatively normal. But then something catches his eye. A warning sign that not all is right. His heart pounds rapidly in his chest. He grabs his coat and runs for the door; he frantically twists the knob but it seems to be jammed, trapping him inside. Fortunately, as he hears the shower turn off, he flips the deadbolt and escapes.

What was the telltale sign? No, it was not the head in the fridge, though that didn't lend any reassurance. It was what Bruce saw in his trick's CD rack. The full collection of Hole CDs left only one possibility—he had stumbled into the lair of a Courtney Love queen. Bruce knew that a fan of the Diva Love is the praying mantis of the gay world: a dangerous, chemically-fueled psychopath.

But what other messages can be revealed by a gay man's CD collection? With this quick reference guide tucked in their wallets beside the condoms, gay men can stay safe from all sorts of unknown drama.

Gay men have long worshipped female singers. According to legend, the 1969 Stonewall Riots were touched off by the death of Judy Garland. Other old school divas include Barbra, Bette, Aretha, and Dietrich. A young queer guy might try to deny that the diva has a place in his life, but a quick perusal of his CD collection reveals the specter of the Modern Rock Diva.

—The Björk queen is a little faerie prince, fey and sprightly... or so he would have you think. He doesn't want to know that he's not from a volcanic island, but rather Nebraska.

—The Nico queen feels that goths just don't understand the concept of doom. You will catch echoes in his voice of the Nordic wasteland. Sometimes he will laugh a hollow laugh-"Ho ho ho ho"—as though from inside the helmet of a suit of armor.

—The Elizabeth Fraser queen, worshipper of the Cocteau Twins, is spooky at first, then beautiful but incomprehensible. But by the end of the relationship, you can understand him perfectly, and he's calling you toxic. And after breaking up, you can forget about a reunion.

—The Amanda Palmer queen behaves as though he is a coin-operated boy, and is constantly going on about his loyal fanbase, which seems to be what he calls his legion of ex-tricks.

—The Kathleen Hanna queen is a riot boi with a star tattooed on his belly. But he's no different from the rest. And don't let him near a Courtney queen… sparks will fly. Eventually, he will go electro and shack up with a Christina Aguilera queen.

—The Yoko queen knows that John was the untalented one. He will have you participate in pieces from *Grapefruit*… like having you cut his clothes off of him.

—The Diamanda queen is drama itself. Correct playback possible at MAXIMUM volume only.

—The Lady Gaga queen may be too deep in a blackout to even remember your date, slurring out questions like "What's the name of this club?"

And that's only the tip of the iceberg. Proceed with extreme caution should you encounter Taylor Swift queens, Beyoncé queens, or, heaven forefend, Jewel queens. I hesitate to even breathe the rumor that there might be Miley Cyrus queens. I don't wish to soil my mind with imagining what the proclivities of those poor souls might be.

Washed Up Pride Performers

Every year at Gay Pride festivals around the world, there is a need for entertainment. Because gay people have been redefined as a demographic—specifically a demographic with a taste for certain performers—those stars are in demand for appearances at Gay Pride. However, there is an issue in that a limited quantity of money is available for paying performers, despite the sponsorship of corporations. So it's necessary to hire celebrities who are down on their luck, who can't command the money they once did but still have some residual name recognition due to past hits. They are people who haven't charted in 10 years or more, but they still need to eat. They receive some income from their old songs when used in commercials and rerun on VH1, but they can't seem to enjoy a real comeback. They are individuals who perhaps have a loyal following among gay people who liked them when both the musicians and fans were younger.

But who will be the languishing stars of tomorrow? It seems entirely possible that the likes of Britney Spears will not continue to have hits indefinitely. Perhaps she won't be ready for the Gay Pride circuit for 20 years or so. Will Eminem someday have his bills paid for by the people who once decried him? In the future, he'll be a paunchy man with his bleached hair now balding, wearing makeup to cover up his pockmarked face, bitterly reprising the hit songs of his youth for a bunch of sunburned homosexuals.

Marilyn Manson or Courtney Love, not looking any prettier than today, may one day be yelling out, "Do you feel proud, Toledo?" and squawking out versions of their old songs for indifferent audiences of rainbow-clad celebrants while the younger members of the audience wonder who these plastic surgery disasters onstage might be.

The audience will indifferently sip their corporate beer from plastic cups and wander around among the booths wearing perhaps less clothing than is wise. The crowd in front of the stage will be sparse until the has-been finally rolls the backing track of the one hit wonder's wonderful one hit. Then there will be a stampede for the stage as the Gay Pride celebrants rush to witness the tattered remains of a once viable talent.

I wouldn't complain if some of my current favorite musicians were to show up—should their fortunes stall—at a future Gay Day. Even if it means that the performance is marred by sound bleed from the outdoor dance area, harsh sunlight, and the bitter taste of rainbow-tinted career failure.

Publicity Successes and Failures

We all know of people who are talented but not well known, and people who are hacks that are famous. Those of us who troll the cultural depths are willing to fish diligently for talent. There is still an underground source of buzz, of places we go for reviews, of people whose taste we trust.

In my case that would be zines, the small presses, record store email lists, and the recommendations of other bohemians. If more than one trusted person or publication mentions a name, I know to check out the book or music.

Others rely on sources that don't care about what's good, just what's supposed to be selling. I am out foraging for free-range culture but what they are promoting is factory-farmed and force-fed.

Publicity is the job of getting more attention than you would get otherwise. People deserve to have recognition in proportion to their talent. I want to direct the spotlight to people who are getting less glory than their gifts warrant. There are many untalented famous folks. They're pretty or rich or perhaps associate with more talented people. They are also getting coverage because there is money going to a publicist who is reminding the media about this person. There are journalists who, because publicists have forged a bond with them, hype publicity clients. The media is desperate for ideas and can't (or won't) go discover actual talent on its own.

But not everyone gets publicity. There are people who cannot get a buzz going. Musicians with recordings made but unreleased; bands without a manager; artists who have personality quirks that get in the way (or lack the social skills needed to get their music heard). What does it take to get their act together? Others create too-challenging music. People don't want to hear stuff that intense, they want something bland, preferring to be lulled into a sense of sonorous blahdom.

It makes me wonder what will make people turn off the television and leave their houses. I speculate about what the magic formula is, and what sources of information people listen to, where an artist needs to place herself to get attention.

Still, I sometimes end up being more part of the publicity problem than part of the solution. It can be a problem when you know someone who is a pleasant enough person but not producing art that's all that great. The best thing I can come up with is to give them constructive criticism and suggest other art for them to check out in the hope that they will improve. It means I have to recommend more heartily that audiences pay attention to other, more distinguished art. There needs to be a balance of helping people on the one hand, with getting the word out and critique on the other.

We have arrived at culture in quotation marks, a society where award ceremonies honor not those who created the best art but rather those who performed the entertainment which sold the most. The only way this will change is for people to individually and collectively take responsibility for supporting the best art they can find.

Post-Celebrity

What ever happened to famous people? They used to be a lot of them but everyone forgot about them since every town in the world started having an open mike. Now everyone knows the names and voices of everyone in their neighborhood. Now every Sunday everyone on the block goes to the corner cafe and people talk about things that matter to them. Sometimes someone vaguely familiar shows up at some place's open mike, and maybe one or two people remember that that person was once a celebrity. But their performance doesn't seem exceptionally more talented than anyone else's. Nobody bothers to move to Hollywood anymore. You can get known in your own town. You will have all the readers of your writing or listeners to your music you'll ever need. Nobody watches television, nobody even bothers with making local access shows. Why bother with that when you get better feedback at your own corner cafe? Part of traveling is visiting the open mike where you're going and meeting the people there. You can go down to any corner and meet a whole group of people involved with being creative. Everyone is creative. Everyone is a star.

How to be a Good Audience

So many times lately my experience at public performances has been less than optimal due to certain audience members whose behavior is less than ideal. I have been tempted to bring a pillow with which to smother fellow spectators. Audiences just don't know how to behave. Maybe it's the result of a generation being raised on TV and video, where the show is the same regardless of what you do.

The greatest and most common sin is talking. Movie patrons, apparently spoiled by the advent of the DVD and downloads, jabber endlessly during the film. Folks, you are not at home on your couch... but maybe you should be. Please refrain from asking your date what is going to happen next, commenting on the set decoration, or whatever other mindless blather you should really save until the post-movie cup of decaf.

Band audiences can also be annoying. Usually the loud volume of rock serves to drown out most audience chatter but when a band reduces their volume and plays an acoustic number, the audience doesn't seem to make a corresponding reduction in their output. If you must blab during the show, move away from the stage.

The exception to being a quiet audience member is going to a comedy club. They say laughter burns calories. Well, if you go to see live comedy and don't laugh, it's like going to the gym and not working out. If it's funny, give a giggle. But saying you shouldn't be silent doesn't mean you can heckle. A heckler always thinks they're helping to make the show funnier and they're always wrong. If you want to try to do the comedian's job, go to an open mike and get on stage. No matter how many drinks you've had, keep your heckles to yourself.

Why do classical music fans all have the same dry cough? Is it an environmental illness endemic to symphony halls? And the cure—crinkling cellophane coughdrop wrappers—is worse than the disease.

Shifting gears to another sort of concert... slamdancing is a baby that is no longer cute. People will slam to Enya these days. Why must the pit be right in front of the stage? The jocks getting their jollies having a rugby scrum aren't watching the band, so why must they occupy the spot with the best view in the house? Go slam in some corner by the back of the room. Almost as bad are the bitter non-slammers who shove at the edge of the mosh-pits, especially when they shove other bystanders who happen to be thrown off balance by boorish slammers. I see mostly bodyslamming and not much dancing in most mosh pits. I find a good fake seizure will usually calm a mosh pit right down.

Fugazi audiences can be particularly tiresome. There's usually a contingent of morons who don't realize Fugazi has hand-picked the opening acts, who may be rather different from them musically. These fans have musical one-track minds: they say, "Who invited this band?" Just your heroes, Fugazi, you dope. Why doesn't Fugazi get out onstage first and introduce their protégés instead of making them sacrificial victims?

Another specific example: why do people walk out of Andy Warhol movies? Didn't they realize when they bought the tickets that it would be long and dull? What will they be able to do with the remaining hour of their evening that's more worthwhile than looking at some of the great art of the 20th century? Don't they know that one of Warhol's mottos was "leave them wanting less"? Don't they know some things are better in retrospect, but you won't have a retrospect if you don't experience it in the first place? Just think of watching the film as looking at a painting for an hour and a half, without other art patrons getting between you and it.

I hope you've paid attention... it'll be good practice for being attentive next time you're an audience member.

Bands are Dumb

I've spent lots of time seeing other people's rock bands, but those people don't often reciprocate by coming to my events. I know a lot about music. I also know a lot about the not-strictly trivial things that surround music: who was in what band, when records came out, etc. Rock music is not the pinnacle of musical achievement. It is repetitive, uninventive, lacking in dynamics or tempo changes, short on complexity, has few emotional dimensions, and is often played by people with limited techniques... and those are its good points.

I am a classically trained pianist. I rarely listen to classical music, though. Like the poor, classical music will always be with us and I can immerse myself in it later. These days I like pop music that's unpopular—Momus, the Magnetic Fields—music with clever lyrics and well-crafted counterpoint. But music that isn't rock.

I've spent lots of time seeing people's rock bands, people who don't seem to come see the stuff as I do. Maybe that's what made me cranky enough to write this. Rock is right up there with film as an art form that takes a lot of time investment, often without subsequent artistic return on that investment. All that time spent practicing (which in the case of rock doesn't mean improving your technique, just sharing bong-hits with your bandmates and cranking up the volume in a small room smelling of sweatsocks), recording, touring, getting gigs, just for some loud guitars and ringing ears and a blowjob in an alley. A lot of people seem to think it's worth it. They're brainwashed by the idea that they might strike it rich, become rock stars.

Indie rock is a higher state of consciousness than, say, Christina Aguilera fandom, but it sure ain't Zen Buddhism. But a lot of people seem to get frozen into a mediocre indie-rock level of musical competence and knowledge, particularly if they're punk purists of the sort to whom musical innovation is taboo.

I can't believe how many bad rock singles I've heard. If your band can't put out a single with two perfect pop gems, you should break up. No good songs = no good band.

I've complained before about people with bad influences, but there isn't that much difference between Duran Duran (bad) and Big Black (good). None of it is Johannes Brahms. Rock rarely makes you cry or gives you goosebumps. You can't hardly dance to it. It's usually too loud and it has to be because it's so dull that people talk right through the rock show. People go see the same band play the same songs the same way over and over again. Yet they have such short attention spans that can't pay attention to a song longer than four minutes with more than two sections... even a bridge is too far.

Rhetorical question time: how can you justify your band's existence? Your stupid, incompetent musical crap? What's the point of Do-It-Yourself if you're just too unskilled to Do It properly? Are you just pandering to stupid people? Taking away attention that should go to someone more talented? Is it the fault of our educational system for not teaching us to appreciate more complex forms of music? Come on, check out Richard Strauss or Igor Stravinsky or John Coltrane for stuff as intense as hardcore, but with actual musical ideas.

No matter what, rock and other even more annoying forms of music aren't going away. I can only imagine that an ever-descending spiral of musical tripe will be generated in the future. Something to look forward to.

Pop Music

My discovery of pop music didn't occur until college. Somehow I didn't feel free to enter a record store and make purchases the way I did with books. Perhaps it was that the cost of a record was around $7 instead of the $2 or $3 that a book cost. Both of these costs have now at least doubled for a new item... imagine the bigger barrier for impoverished kids today, and it's no wonder online music trading flourishes.

While I didn't listen to the music, I would read newspaper accounts that began my focus on trivia that continues to this day. My constant struggle for up-to-dateness is a compensation for its former lack. The pop music I eventually got into wasn't very popular pop, though. I started listening to the punk bands that my college friends listened to.

That kind of pop music changed my life. Political pop like Beefeater, Minor Threat, and the Minutemen highlighted the personal as political, and influenced life changes and stands. Beefeater members were vegetarians, and I soon became one. (Hey, at least I wasn't following the lead of the Smiths like every other veggie.)

Do politics belong in pop music? Is it just a marketing ploy? Examples in commercial pop: the Tibet occupation that the Beastie Boys have featured, medical benefits, PETA ads, playing at inaugurations, lyrics about domestic abuse, runaways, feminism, anti-racist actions, against police brutality, etc. Certainly words that question commercialism are more rare in commercial rock. There are even anti-corporate postures taken by rockers like Tom Morello and Serj Tankian who released music on corporate labels.

Because of the backwards way I got into pop music, there are still many more popular pieces of music that I haven't heard, even though I'm familiar with other very obscure songs. I've never spent much time listening to mainstream radio or watching music videos. In some ways my musical education has happened in reverse; I would seek out earlier music based on its influence on later music that I liked.

Perhaps my attention and listening time would have been better spent on more complex musical forms like jazz or classical music. Even though I should know better by now, my record collection is largely composed of pop recordings.

I like music with ideas, whether those thoughts are embodied in the music itself in the form of innovations, game rules like Brian Eno's *Oblique Strategies*, references, collage, or in the lyrics where they may be biographical, political, storytelling, etc. While there can be appeal in pop music which lacks originality in both music and lyrics, any pleasure in listening is outweighed by shame.

It's Not Easy Being an Arrogant Know-It-All

Having to constantly suffer the company of the ignorant, it's difficult to suppress my condescension. After all, I know about obscure music and books that few others know of and this makes me superior.

For that matter, I must also tolerate the naive with regard to politics and current events. It is a constant struggle to maintain a civil façade, to avoid an outburst. After all, the polite response to the uninformed is not to point out their glaring faults but to gently correct their errors in a subtle, guiding way. Maintaining patience is not easy.

I was talking the other day to an acquaintance (it's hard for people to actually be friends with one as superior as me) and I was shocked to find he'd never heard of Sainkho Namtchylak. Come on, what rock do you have to be living under to not know of the Tuvan throat-singing virtuoso—a singer who makes Diamanda Galas sound like Whitney Houston—who collaborates with free-jazzers like saxophonist Evan Parker? I tried not to be too disdainful as I informed him of her numerous releases on the British record label, Leo. It's just so difficult not to get sarcastic when faced with that sort of colossal ignorance and cultural complacency.

Do these people just take whatever is offered them on MTV, instead of digging deeper? I have to laugh at the people who think they're hip just because they listen to something they consider obscure, like Borbetomagus. Come on, they've been around forever. Even some grunge-listening moron who hasn't picked up a magazine since Forced Exposure turned into a mail-order company knows that.

How did I become as I am: namely, one of the most hip people on the planet, endowed with a broad cultural knowledge? Obscurantists are made, not born. To tell the wounding truth, my strength came from weakness. In high school, I was a geek, woefully ignorant of popular culture and rock music in particular. My reading was predominantly in the genre of science fiction. I listened to the folk and classical music my parents preferred and, for exoticism's sake, enjoyed the synthesizer stylings of Wendy Carlos and Tomita. Children have no taste. We're shaped (or should I say twisted?) by our environment.

Once I discovered punk rock, I shot up like a late bloomer whose delayed pubescence doesn't preclude his growth to a height greater than six feet. I devoured the *Trouser Press Record Guide*, listened to lots of music from the collections of friends. I started reading obscure magazines that reviewed music none of my friends listened to and I was an early adopter of the Internet: I had email in college in 1984 and my Usenet newsgroup posts archived on Google Groups date back that far, before the 1987 Great Renaming, which reorganized online discussion forums. I was an invited member of a secret email music list called "Music-flamers" in 1986.

Let's face it, it's too easy to put someone down for being a fan of Korn or Britney Spears (what's the difference, really?). I prefer to insult people for being so obvious as to be fans of virtually mainstream 1970s British psyche-folk group Caravan instead of Everyone Involved or fill-in-the-blank with your favorite ultra-obscure, private pressing, un-reissued psyche-folk LP of the early '70s.

Why should music be something that we have in common, something that might bring us together, when it can be a soapbox to stand on to put us above other people? Why settle for the pleasure of turning on someone to good music when you can use it to put them down? If you can tell me, I'll let you listen to my copy of Jim French and Galas's *If Looks Could Kill* or Orchid Spangiafora's *Flee Past's Ape Elf*.

VI. On Homosexuality

The International Homosexual Conspiracy

The International Homosexual Conspiracy is as old as human history. It may predate the earliest recorded gay couple, manicurists of an Egyptian Pharaoh. Ancient Greeks like Socrates, Plato, and Sappho participated. Jesus and the Apostles were members. Guys in beards and dresses performing sex magic with John the Baptist. Closet queen Paul repressed the queer teachings (evil right-wing closet case lawyer Roy Cohn was his reincarnation). Monks of the Carmina Burana kept it alive in the Dark Ages. Minstrels, tellers of the Tarot, Gilles de Rais, Joan of Arc: agents of the conspiracy. Walt Whitman, Oscar Wilde, (okay, so I skipped hundreds of years in there), and so on. Finally, Magnus Hirschfeld and his archives. He was the mastermind of the 20th century explosion of homosexuality. Harry Hay and the secret Mattachine Society. All the Gay Liberation Fronts and Queer Nations since that time.

The International Homosexual Conspiracy is not something you're recruited into. You're born with the predilections that make you a natural part of it. You're already a stealth member before you even know it. You're contacted by agents who may not know they're agents themselves. They initiate you into the rites of the conspiracy, which you think are instinctual… because they are. The conspiracy is programmed into you. You live out the conspiracy. That's the beauty of it. The mastermind of the conspiracy is a gene.

But in the modern age (with props to Karl Heinrich Ulrichs and Edward Carpenter), Hirschfeld was among the first to recognize what might be termed homosexual proclivity. He had an interest in eugenics, ironic in that he was ultimately persecuted by the Nazis. He decided to shape the ends of this propensity to his own purposes.

The societal purpose of the homosexual gene has been to improve the situation of the family related to the individual carrying the genetic trait. The gene is somewhat recessive, probably occurring in several chromosomes to become dominant. Happens to 10 percent, so they say. It's beneficial to the family in societies like the historical Zuni Indians. They had a sex-role integrated into society for the homosexual or gender-crossing individual; the person stayed with the mother's family, did women's work. An analogous role would be taken by some genetic females. Without the pressures of kids of their own, they have the chance to contribute to the existing extended families.

Hirschfeld predicted the fall of the nuclear family unit, arguing that there would be greater independence for the individual of any sexuality but at the cost of an individual's weakening due to loss of the old family support. For the previous century, homosexuality had been manifesting itself in individuals such as Wilde: solitary homosexuals who did fine until their rock was overturned and they were exposed to the power of society embodied in the vindictive justice system. Hirschfeld saw that homosexuals must begin to band together. This would enable the interdependent homosexuals to be stronger than the newly isolated heterosexuals.

Now the homosexual conspiracy was becoming more than a conspiracy of nature, of genetics, than it had been. Now it was a conspiracy with concerted thinking behind it.

One research finding has been to show the genetic nature of homosexuality. In fact, Freud aside, genetics are much more important than environment as a predictor of homosexuality. The classic study shows that if a person has a queer sibling, one is more likely to be queer oneself. And the closer the blood relationship, the better. In identical twins raised together, almost 100% have the same sexuality. Raised apart, slightly lower (but I bet one's a closet case). Fraternal, slightly lower again, and so forth but being related is the greatest correlation. If this knowledge was common to heterosexuals, they might want to get rid of this "abnormality," actually a positive adaptation over millennia of evolution. And you don't mess with Mutha Nature.

But with the homosexual conspiracy, a method of concentrating this genetic potential to make a race of super-queers seems an obvious result. There is the potential to make queers into an ethnic group. Already, go into a gay bar and observe the similarities in appearance. Homosexuals like to think themselves a diverse group but they actually have a small gene pool. It's likely that there isn't just one form of genetic homosexuality. We already may be able to observe this: one could conjecture that there's a bear gene, a twink gene, and so on. The use of gay sperm donors by lesbians may result in a strain of more or less true-breeding homosexuals. Note that there have been recent moves under the pretext of AIDS prevention to ban the use of sperm donated by gay men.

The goal of my revelation is not that the conspiracy be overthrown but that those who have been unwitting participants can know about the process. Band together with your fellow homosexuals and create a new and better society. Long live the International Homosexual Conspiracy!

I Want to be a Gay Wingnut

San Francisco has its share of wingnuts: questionably sane people who feel compelled to bring their offbeat beliefs to a public forum. The guy who holds a sign saying aliens want to impeach the president (it used to read Clinton, then Bush, now Van Buren); the guy who proclaims the Dalai Lama's a cannibal; the guy who believes Stephen King killed John Lennon.

In that way, I want to bring my beliefs to gay people, whether they want to hear them or not. Other gay people have driven me that crazy.

I'm going to make big signs with my slogans (DISCO CAUSES BRAIN CANCER ... BAN GAY CLONING ... GOING TO THE GYM MEANS LESS TIME FOR ART). I'll make badly typewritten manifestos, with odd diagrams in the corners. I'll have a bullhorn to announce my rants beneath the large rainbow flag in the Castro. I want to cultivate a wild-eyed stare, an uncomfortable manner, and bad body odor. I want to fax newspapers letters full of crackpot theories.

Either by force, or by disguising myself as a spandex-and-mirrorshades DJ with a crate of records, I barricade myself in the DJ booth of San Francisco's biggest and most vacuous disco. Hordes of drugged-out mindless gymbots gyrate to whatever's still spinning on the turntable, not a thought in their heads. I pull the plug, and the record shows down: *eeeer... thud—thud—thud...* They come halfway out of their trance, looking confused like zombies in a horror film after the zombie master dies.

Hah! But I am the new zombie master. My voice echoes out loud over the speakers, booms from the giant woofers designed to shake bowels and numb brains. And this is what I say, in a voice colored with haughty self-righteousness:

"For too long, you have escaped responsibility, escaped meaning, escaped culture, escaped everything that ought to bring purpose to existence... instead filling yourselves with drugs, pointless sex, the gym, music with all the complexity of a car alarm, and the ceaseless worship of your own vanity. But I am now holding up a mirror not to your faces but to your souls. The circuit party is like the repetitive track worn by Shetlands shackled to the cross-arms of a county fair pony ride.

"For too long, a tiny cadre of activists has worked to fight injustice without your help. For too long, a loyal audience has supported live performance while you were a slave to canned rhythm. It's time for you to do your part."

But I know it's futile. Their minds are as barricaded as Fort Knox and only hitting some sort of cultural rock bottom will ever bring them out of it. No therapy I can offer would be sufficiently shocking.

Closet Case Role Models

All queers are former closet cases but most of us came out before we got famous. I'm speaking specifically of certain celebrities featured at major gay events such as national marches on Washington. The rosters are a veritable *Who's Who* of people who were once notorious closet cases... and even, in at least some cases, still are, if rumors are to be believed.

So why are we treating these people—who got where they are today partially through dishonesty—as role models, when the true role models are individuals around us who have been facing the world as openly gay people for a lot longer than certain celebrities?

If public figures are going to be handed a gig with such symbolic importance, why not invite musicians, comedians, and politicians who have been out throughout their careers? While there's no denying that in most cases the recently out stars have talent, their fame is partially due to falsely taken straight privilege. In contrast are the talented open queers who perhaps could have had more successful careers had they not been so open.

We've seen this career path repeated more than once: someone early on performs in local gay venues, women's music festivals, and so on, never really making a big statement but not refusing the stage time. Then there's a period of eschewing that path, seeking mainstream success, climbing the mainstream entertainment ladder. They become famous and then there are rumors, tabloid stories, but no direct comment, unless it's overt denial. Eventually the celebrity decides to come out. There is a big splash, a dip as some homophobic fans rush out, disgusted that they considered themselves a fan of that revolting homo, while the gay media and some of the gay public rally around the celebrity who is now "their" icon. After an initial blush, the celeb decides again that they don't want to have their celebrity be all about their sexuality, and there is another period of de-gaying, where gay content is downplayed. There may be some middle-of-the-road gay political involvement, but nothing radical.

The alternative path follows someone who is involved with the gay community all along. The person may not get signed to a major label or get television time. A performer may be exploited by Gay Pride celebrations that expect free performances. Critics may say that their art doesn't reflect universal experience, and they are presented as not of interest to straight people.

A gay politician may not be able to get elected to wider office because of constituent homophobia while closet cases ascend to the Senate before being outed amid protestations that their sexuality is irrelevant to their politics.

Privilege is getting ahead by dint of background, connections, and even dishonesty rather than by talent alone. Bitterness is cynicism brought about by having less success than those who have taken a less principled path.

As long as there remains some stigma attached to homosexuality, as long as art with queer content is considered marginal, this pattern will be repeated. Ironically, these late-blooming former closet cases may finally do some marginal good and make it less likely that this pusillanimous route will be taken in the future.

Presumed Hetero Until Proven Gay

In our unrelievedly heterosexist society, we live under the illusion that heterosexuality is the default. We assume the people whom we meet are heterosexual until they are proven—either by their own admission or by the testimony of other reliable witnesses—to be gay.

The reasons for wanting to know someone's sexuality include wanting to have sex with them, or wanting to engage in political or cultural activities with them that is predicated on identity. One wants to know if someone shares cultural reference points based on sexuality.

Imagine instead the results if we made other assumptions about people's sexuality… that they are presumed to be queer unless proven straight. Yes, even the people pushing strollers or holding hands with people who appear to be genetically of the other societally-described gender. We could assume all people are bisexual. In a place like San Francisco, where everyone is open and liberal and unlikely to be insulted about being mistaken for gay, or may even have similar cultural reference points, it's no big deal to assume people are gay even if you make occasional mistakes.

If two people are of the same gender and are together (and I'm getting gay vibes from one and not the other), I use guilt by association to implicate them both as homosexuals. We could go out and experiment. See if anyone threatens to be violent.

When I've been leafleting for a queer cause in a not exclusively gay scene like an antiwar protest, there have been people who've given me the how-dare-you-assume-that-I'm-gay attitude, even when I'm trying to target people who are clearly in a homosexual circle of friends or are wearing rainbow pins or flags. People who are clearly identifying. I need to work more on my own identifying characteristics, like wearing a pin or something. Despite the fact that my body language is not traditionally masculine, I still meet gay people who don't figure out that I'm queer right away.

Why can't we just all assume we're bisexual? People view heterosexuality as some sort of virtue. Whether someone is gay or straight, to be perceived as heterosexual makes someone better. To be called gay-looking is considered insulting, even to gay people.

Society's consensus: a man who harbors attraction for other men is less than fully a man; likewise for women. Queers are damaged.

How can we overcome this presumption and reach some sort of omnisexual utopia? People feel they have to hide their love away. If platonic love can be shown, that's a first step. Let's hear it for those cultures where men walk hand in hand as they talk walking down the street.

Heterosexual vs. Straight-identified

It's okay to be heterosexual but please don't be straight-identified. Asserting and maintaining a straight identity is inherently homophobic. It's defining oneself as non-gay. Relax already.

Much more palatable are the post-straights. They realize that "straight" is a socially constructed category, not an inherent trait. These people admit that they are not just suburban missionary positioners but they also aren't trying to be grabby by claiming "queer" without being at least somewhat homo.

There's something even worse than straight-identified people who actually are heterosexual: people who want to claim heterosexual privilege without doing the dirty work of touching the genitals of a different biological sex. This lousy cadre includes closeted celebrities, religion-damaged self-denialists, old-school "curious" guys, and new-school down-low thugs. Perhaps these people are doing some good by eroding the currency of straight identity but they are not really fooling anyone beside themselves.

The postmodern heterosexual has a careful line to tread: to appear gay-friendly without looking gay; to look sexually available without appearing to posture lewdly. Formerly, only non-straight sexual minorities had to use secret codes of hankies and keys and stickers but now that heterosexuals are a sexual minority as well, they must rapidly accelerate the development of their own signifiers.

Unfortunately, many of the signs that heterosexuals use to indicate their liberation are appropriated from homosexuals. Witness the straight guys with bleached hair, piercings, thumb-rings, and necklaces. That sort of thing isn't helping anyone—it's confusing to both gays and straights. Gay guys end up hitting on the haplessly stylish hetero, and straight girls write him off as yet another homo. I'm willing to make an exception for straight guys wearing "Nobody Knows I'm a Lesbian" shirts. That points in the right direction. Breeder dudes *should* be appropriating from lesbians, not from gay men. And hetero women should be stealing from faggots. Let's see more chicks in tacky International Male garb and dudes featuring double-headed axe necklaces. And strap-ons all around.

Mixed nightclubs where gays and straights mingle end up being downright confusing when you can't tell the difference between the players. The postmodern maxim is that sexual identity doesn't matter, it's just about who will have sex with you. Or not have sex with you. And if the heteros are hip to Leigh Bowery and the homos groove to Captain Beefheart, you can have a reasonable conversation with anybody in the joint, whether it's a homo sporting retro-straight fashions or a hetero in retro-gay style.

In the future, the current modes of sexuality will seem as quaint as the 19th century homosexual terms Uranian and Tribade. Our current alphabet of identities will all be passé. Perhaps there will be new labels but, more likely, people will simply not bother with labels any longer.

Confrontation

This is a story about the first time I confronted homophobia. In the mid-'80s, when I was a college student at St. Olaf in Minnesota, a group of campus jocks silkscreened t-shirts with a logo featuring a stylized icon of two men having anal sex with a circle and slash over them. This resulted in a series of Letters to the Editor about the shirts, and apparently in response to the letters, the guys stopped wearing the shirts... for the most part, at least. About a year later, I was in the college cafeteria and spotted a guy wearing one of the shirts. I carried my tray to another table and sat down, but I was seething and I couldn't abide to do nothing.

I had attended a workshop about harassment (at the other, more liberal college in town), presented by the campus Lesbian and Gay group. A lesbian and a gay man came to talk and teach us about confronting harassment. They offered a four-part formula— 1) Label it: say "That's harassment." 2) Express displeasure: "I don't like it." 3) Back it up: "Nobody likes it." 4) Tell them to quit: "Stop it." All together now: "That's harassment. I don't like it. Nobody likes it. Stop it."

So I decided to confront the guy, shame him in front of the woman he was eating dinner with. I stood by their table, my knees shaking, my voice unsteady. I didn't exactly follow the script.

"I can't believe you're eating with a guy who would wear a shirt like that," I said to the blond woman sitting across the table from the jock. She giggled and looked down at her tray uncomfortably. "Take that shirt off and give it to me," I said. He didn't comply. There was a hush in the cafeteria during my confrontation.

He responded with some smartass comment. After I stalked away, a few of my friends congratulated me. I never saw the guy wear the shirt again.

The Prime Directive

I'm in a gay bar in Iowa. How I got here: I was going to my brother's college graduation in rural western Illinois. I got the bored feeling that I wanted to go to a gay bar. There were none in town that I knew of. I'd looked up the region online and found out there were some in Davenport Iowa, across the border around an hour away.

I drove through the near-deserted interstate and found Davenport and managed to navigate to the bar. It was in a fairly deserted area. As I parked my car I saw a disheveled woman whom I assumed was a streetwalker. I always like to flatter myself that I'm straight-acting enough that prostitutes will solicit me anyway, and I'll get to tell them something sassy like "Sorry, I'm a faggot." She didn't say anything to me.

I show my California ID at the front desk and pay the cover.

Inside there's a bar to the right and a stairway up to the left. Under the stairway is a wide opening to the dance floor room, which has a raised stage towards the front of the building. Towards the back is a passage that leads to a patio area. Part of this has an awning. There are tables. There is even a sand volleyball court. There is a wooden stairway going up to a second-floor deck. There's a door back inside from the deck which leads to the same room as the stairway inside the front door, and this room has a pool table and a CD jukebox. There's a high fence around the backyard of the bar. Off the balcony I can see the parking lot behind another tavern on the other side of the block.

There are a lot of people in the bar. They look pretty normal for the most part. Fairly young. Some are probably college students. There's an older guy holding court at the front room bar. A drag show is going to be starting soon and there are a couple of queens in the room.

I don't talk to anyone all night. I'm not nervous. But I feel as though I'm exercising the Prime Directive as if on *Star Trek*. I don't want to disturb their way of life with my weird West Coast worldview. I could be time-traveling back to my own Midwestern '80s days. There is nothing out of date or contemporary, it's just somewhere vaguely in the last two decades of the 20th Century. There are a few guys with tattoos. They're talking with groups of friends. I don't want to bust in. I have some of my stickers for my website, which I stick on a railing of the balcony. I guess that's violating the prime directive. I also drop a few back issues of my zine *Holy Titclamps* around.

I could easily go and make a fool of myself because I'm never going to see any of these people again. I could do something that could change someone's life. I could even cheat on my boyfriend and nobody would ever know. I could be completely anonymous or do something that would make people talk here for weeks. I could strip nude on the dance floor. I could call the police and have the place shut down. I could start a fight. But I do none of these things. I just wander around and look at people. I guess I'm being creepy. I'm sure these people generally recognize fellow regulars and know that I'm not one of them.

Finally I leave this bar and go to the other gay bar two doors down. This place is more like a wood-paneled saloon. There's a karaoke machine, not currently in use. People are gathered around the horseshoe bar. There's a stage. I see a flyer indicating that a gay ventriloquist for whom I produced a show in San Francisco is performing here the following week. The clientele in this bar seems a little older, and it's a little more conducive to talking than the dance bar. Somewhere else in town is a leather bar, which is probably where the bears are, since they don't seem to be present much here. Still, I follow the prime directive and don't talk to people. I do leave a few copies of my zine by the free newspaper rack, wondering what people might think of it here.

I finally decide to give up on Iowa and drive back to Illinois. I had a chance to make my changes on a micro scale, and I missed it. Someday maybe I can come back to Iowa and try to make my mark again.

Clones are Good

Clones are a popular punching bag, one that I've hit myself more than once. There are various subcultures, including some forms of gays, who have a tendency to dress and look the same. The first group to which the term "clone" was attached was the 1970s gays with the look of mustaches and tight jeans. There was a "new clone" look of the ACT UP/Queer Nation years of the late '80s and early '90s, with leather jackets sporting brightly colored sticker slogans. But if we look even at earlier photos of various sorts of gays, we see groups of similar-looking people: bulldykes in suits; sweater- and clamdigger-clad Fire Island pioneers; motorcycle-straddling bikers.

Clones provide visibility and build movements. The members of the group can identify each other. People must gain some benefit from this visual conformity or it would not happen. People are able to get social benefits such as sexual and social success by adopting a uniform look. A more recent form of clone is the bear subculture where beards, flannel, and a husky body type produce a new image of the homosexual man.

The reason that clones are supposed to be bad is that they are a syndrome of conformity. Individuality is held up as an ideal. The exterior uniformity of clones reflects an internal uniformity and lack of creative thought. The clones are all supposed to like the same sort of music and have a standardized set of beliefs.

In the opinion of this amateur sociologist, clones tend to be only similar in physical appearance but have individual views. For example, some bears like punk rock while others prefer house music. While attributing individual consciousness to wearers of Abercrombie and Fitch fashions may be a far stretch, the possibility exists that they are able to entertain unique thoughts occasionally.

The eradication of clones is likely a futile hope but, while there is little prospect for complete diversity of individuals, we can hope for biodiversity in the form of a larger number of coexisting clone species. There is always the possibility that some subgroup of an existing clone form may split off and become a viable clone form on its own, or that perhaps the characteristics of more than one clone group may combine in a new one (e.g., musclebears, which are a sort of hybrid of gym queens and bears).

The origin of clone species is somewhat in question. Perhaps the bears of today are the mustachioed clones of the '70s, simply grown older, paunchier, and hairier. The popularization of various clone-forms has to do with visual representations of the clones in media, including pornography. *Bear* magazine, for instance, was vital in popularizing the bear look and identity. Commercialization of the look doesn't hurt either, whether it's selling preppie wear, leather harnesses, or identity-related hats and t-shirts.

Clones are here to stay and, as the cliché goes, if you can't beat 'em, join 'em. If you don't feel like merging with any of the existing clone groups, create your own look, talk a few friends into joining in, and start a new clique of inbred conformists.

Gay Male Ignorance of Lesbian Culture

Gay men pay only the barest of lipstick service to dyke culture. They remain ignorant of so many aspects of lesbian culture… nearly as ignorant as straights.

A couple years back I was at a book fair, and members of a panel of gay and lesbian writers complained about how straight people weren't reading their books. In the comment period, I stood up and angrily said that the people not reading gay and lesbian books were right here in this room: gay men who didn't read Sarah Schulman, Blanche McCrary Boyd, Jewelle Gomez, Carol Anshaw, Michelle Tea, et al. I can't as easily recommend gay male writers to lesbians, since much gay male writing is crap that would be ignored were it not for identity politics marketing.

Sure, there are gay men who read the lesbian comic strip *Dykes to Watch Out For* every two weeks, who have JD Samson pinup calendars, who headbang to The Haggard, who go to Sister Spit readings, who get Marga Gomez's jokes. But many remain ignorant.

Any man who asks, "What do lesbians do in bed?" would no doubt be a lousy lay. If he can't imagine anything beyond some variation on the missionary position, who would want to have sex with him? Similarly, who would want to have cultural intercourse with someone who was ignoring great art, music and writing by lesbians?

Even though I count myself as one who understands most lesbian cultural references, that doesn't make me comfortable criticizing lesbians the way I do gay male culture. No, I'm enough of an outsider not to critique mullets, serial monogamy, separatism, the lesbian baby boom, Hollywood or Washington, DC power couples, dolphin-shaped dildos, labrys jewelry, etc. That's better left to some tart-tongued lesbian scribe.

I'm one of those gay guys raised by lesbians. I first came out to a straight woman because I knew she had a lesbian friend to whom she could introduce me. When I started going to Carleton College's gay support group, there were lesbians among its leadership. I've always kept up-to-date on music, writing, and comics created by lesbians. Gay male and lesbian culture are two parallel lifestyles, in some ways mirror images of each other. Both are distinct from heterosexual society and also from each other; two different cultural expressions of sexuality, shaped by differing mainstream societal expectations of men and women.

One of my most controversial rants posted online was about misogynist gay men. One of the problems is that people didn't realize that it was written as satire. They wrote to protest that they or their gay male friends are not like that at all. Yet I still encounter men for whom these beliefs are not parody: a gay man who generalizes that he hates all lesbians "because they want to be men;" another uses the word "cunt" to refer to a woman he has no good reason to insult.

Gay men have things to learn from lesbians. Not just how to have serially monogamous relationships and fix motorized vehicles, but how to have sexual politics. Gay men are like the over-commercialized USA, and lesbians are like mellower Canada. Shared, parallel history. Another country that's similar, different... but somehow a little bit better.

My Gender Identity Crisis

I used to think I was a lesbian. It was the U-Haul, the cats, the herbal tea, the flannel, the sobriety, the vegetarianism, the mullet, the peace activism, the sandals, the Sarah Schulman books, not using antiperspirant, the *Hothead Paisan* t-shirt, the poetry readings, my political correctness, the *Girljock* sticker on my bike helmet. I'd rather see Tribe 8 than go to a disco. Rather go to bars like the Lexington than the Midnight Sun in the Castro. All the evidence seemed to be there for my lesbian identity.

More proof: I never wear dresses. But I ain't no lipsticker. Won't find me at Dinah Shore in a pantsuit sipping white wine in the bleach blond hair I don't have. Though I wasn't a femme, I didn't seem to be even a very, very soft butch, either. So somehow lesbian identities weren't totally fitting me.

Until I discovered a new set of role models. This time, they're guys... trans guys to be specific; guys who are comfortable in their masculinity in a way that I've never been. To paraphrase *Car Wash*: these guys are more man than I'll ever be, and have been more woman than I'll ever get.

After a long period of reflection and self-examination, I've turned a corner. I might be not just a boy-dyke but F2M. I guess I could be M2M, though that sounds more like an old AOL chatroom than a gender identity.

Sure, transition would be easy for me: I don't need to inject hormones since I make them on my own; I'm skinny enough that top surgery isn't really necessary; and for bottom surgery or packing, I've got that covered though maybe a little prosthetic addition wouldn't hurt.

I have to work on my presentation. I could probably pass. I am a little different in stature. My facial hair is coming in a little sparse. Maybe I should test the waters by trying to perform as a drag king.

I'm probably a transfag rather than a wannabe straight man. My lesbianism was always pretty platonic. My male lesbian lover will probably stick with me through this transition. I'll probably discover what others have found before me though: transitioning won't help you escape lesbian bed death, it just becomes FTM bed death.

This transition doesn't mean I'm going to be any less of a feminist than I was before. I refuse to accept male privilege. I won't be in the closet, everyone will know about my transition. I'll still be supportive of women's rights and reproductive freedom and lesbian culture. I'll still listen to music by lesbians, read lesbian authors, and religiously follow Dykes To Watch Out For. But I'm also about recognizing a new set of transman heroes expanding the artistic palette.

One advantage will be that there will be no more embarrassing incidents of being chided for using the "wrong bathroom." Turns out people were right to enforce those rigid gender roles on me all along.

Sure, people are going to accuse me of jumping on a trend. Know that I'm not just following the pack but uncovering an innate identity that has slumbered within me all along. I was born male (I think), and dammit, I'm going to embrace that fully and live as such. That doesn't mean I'm going to go around swaggering like some sort of macho asshole. I'm going to transcend the bio-man and emulate the best example of the latest modern model of masculinity, namely, the transman.

Pronouns

Pronouns still have gender, even if people don't much anymore. No matter how liberated someone is, you can't call them "it." That makes them into an object, and nobody wants to be objectified.

But sometimes you just don't know what pronoun to use. When you're meeting someone for the first time, or seeing them again after the passage of time, you find yourself sometimes unsure of what pronoun to use. Someone who answered to one pronoun last week may be insulted by its use this week. So we find elaborate ways to manipulate syntax to avoid using pronouns. For example, repeating the person's name, referring to them by their role, for instance, "the bassist" or "the cook," or saying "that person."

Luckily, when addressing someone directly you rarely have to refer to gender since you don't use the third person. It's when you have to talk about the person to someone else that the problem arises. Gender is a conspiracy between people regarding how individuals are going to be referenced.

And then there are people who ask us to use gender-neutral pronouns like ze and se. It can make one feel like one's in an Esperanto class or a science fiction story. It's respectful to refer to people by the gender presentation they choose and using the pronouns they request. If you say something else, you're implicitly disputing their self-image.

Fortunately, English is already a fairly androgynous language. It is different from most other Indo-European languages that assign genders to inanimate objects (something English seems to want to do to only a few things, like calling ships "she.") It also doesn't have a difference between the way the language is spoken by men and women as do languages like Japanese. On the other hand, the way Japanese is spoken by someone could give clues as to how they identify since, for instance, there is a first person pronoun, "ore", usually only used by males.

The use of the plural pronoun for individuals is sloppy though. If I hear one more person talking about what "they" have been doing, I'm going to bellow at "them."

Even the more liberal Christians are getting in on the act, using gender-neutral language to refer to God since the deity has recently jumped on the post-gender bandwagon... or perhaps has always been on it, with those long flowing dresses and facial hair.

Perhaps every gathering should have a designated gender oracle to whom each arriving guest confides his, her, or hir gender *du jour* so that other guests may retrieve this information without embarrassment, or nametags could be provided with a space to note preferred form of address. However, this makes it sound like people with ambiguous gender are the problem rather than identifying the real problem as the gender system.

I try to save people embarrassment by giving hints when introducing people, for instance, using what I think are people's preferred pronouns: "This is John, and he's a photographer." I will also try to discreetly correct errors of gender identification. Some people insist on loudly and rudely asking, "Is that a man or a woman?" Last time someone did that, my response was "Grow up." If all else fails, just keep buying the person drinks until a bathroom break is necessary. Then watch whether the male- or female-designated facility is used. You'll have the answer you desire, you gender-binary-fixated fossil.

Finding a Man

People are always being offered my unsolicited advice on finding a boyfriend so I thought I'd offer that advice in a public forum where it can do the greatest good for the greatest number. Let's set aside, for the present moment, such timeless unanswerable questions as whether or not homosexuals are actually capable of dating, and get down to the nuts and bolts of finding a man... and keeping him once you've got him.

Kidnapping is one method of getting a man that is not to be ruled out. If you can't get a man voluntarily, try taking one. Since you're probably a typical wimpy fag, physically overpowering him is likely out of the question. Use a chemical to help you out—get hold of some roofies, go to a bar or other place where men are drinking, and pick a target. It's best to pick someone who's not so huge you can't move him yourself, unless you have an accomplice who's willing to double-date with you. Slip some of the chemical in his drink, and once he gets drowsy, guide him out of the bar and to your dungeon. Chain him up, and either wait for him to wake up or just have sex with him as he is, if you prefer the dead type. If you decide to break up, just kill and dismember him. As tempting as it might be to keep a memento of a past love affair, always destroy the head and hands.

Gay bars are a lousy place to meet men. You never know when some random pickup is going to turn out to be a psychopath. It's a kill-or-be-killed world out there, and it's always more blessed to give than receive with it comes to lethal stabbings. Just as if you're a bottom you want to avoid picking up another bottom, if you're a murderer you should avoid going home with another killer.

It's a good idea to pick up guys who don't have a lot of connections with family or friends so there won't be many people following the trail. Dating rich guys has its dangers, because chances are greater that police will follow up or families will hire private investigators. Remember: eat low on the food chain.

It's up to you if you're going to have a one-night stand or a long-term relationship. Having a series of one-night stands may seem easier than having a live-in lover, but remember, if you have a boyfriend you can have sex whenever you want, whereas you might not always get lucky with finding casual pick-ups.

There are problems with long-term relationships: the neighbors may hear him screaming; you'll have to feed him; you need to hose him down so his fetid odor doesn't disgust you.

It's so unfair that there's such a double standard with homosexual and heterosexual relationships. Everyone's always so overjoyed when a man and a woman get hitched but if you tell people you've got a man chained up in your basement, you may actually get thrown in jail. And just forget about getting domestic partner benefits for your sex slave. Sadly, it's still wisest to be in the closet about your relationship. Maybe one day society will be enlightened enough that you can live your lifestyle openly. Now go out there and get yourself a man!

Masculine Men

We've all seen personal ads specifying that the person is looking for a masculine man. Isn't "masculine man" a redundancy? If we say that masculine men are preferred, what do we mean, and what are our assumptions? That there are some defined presumptions about men's characteristics and that men who more strongly bear those traits are preferred? It may also imply that those men who are "feminine" warrant disapproval.

Instead of using stereotypes about what men and women are supposed to be ideally, think of positive and negative traits without stereotypes.Positive traits include taking care of people, talking with people, protecting the weak, cooking, honesty, pleasant personality, etc. Negative traits include violent behavior, greed, arrogance, ill temper, dishonesty. None of these traits are essential to either men or women—all are found to some degree or other in all people.

Essentialists come in various flavors: those who assume all women are naturally nurturing earthmothers; those who believe that men are born to be in charge—and they're all wrong. Generalizers, stereotypers, prejudicers. You can't assume (or rather, you can... but it's asinine).

Some people also think that possessing secondary sexual characteristics in abundance—such as body or facial hair, musculature, or large breasts—makes one more of a man or more of a woman. Hogwash. Being more like a stereotype doesn't make you a better person. Whether you're naturally endowed with some extra hormones or you've been acquiring them elsewhere, you're still just a human not some sort of oversexed demigod! Put something on over that tanktop, for goodness sake!

An acceptable defense may be that someone simply prefers people who fall within a certain range of physical characteristics. That's fine when choosing sexual partners—after all, nobody can have sex with every other person in the world. But to limit your social friendships based on physical characteristics or behavior is an inexcusable form of prejudice.

The Feeling is Mutual: In Praise of Hand Jobs

Mutual masturbation. It sounds like an insurance company but it's actually more pleasurable than that. Masturbation can come in handy. I assume that any male who has had sexual contact with another man has at least on some occasion had this sort of pleasure: his hand touching another man's penis, and that man's hand touching his. This can be assumed even more than any other act. Everyone does this but very few think of it as the peak of what they want to do.

It's part of foreplay preceding some sort of penetrative act or it's used in a situation where the full monty cannot be achieved: masturbated under a coat on a train, reaching under a table, in a bathroom or dormitory. There is an association with the games of youths. Guys just experimenting, the circle jerk over a stolen Playboy turns to the point where guys consent to touch each other. That's a fantasy since I never participated in a circle jerk, just looked at the magazines at a cafeteria table. My friends wouldn't admit to masturbating but I'm sure that they did. Liars!

There is a certain feeling of Huck Finn camaraderie, a Walt Whitman poem. Mutual masturbation is as American as a handshake. Manly: two youths or two men doing the same to each other, at the same time or taking turns. The chakras are in line. None of that strange power juxtaposition that occurs with the French or Greek acts. But the intimacy is at arms' length—there is an embrace but no penetration. It's something that two people can share who have just met or who have known each other for years. It's following the Golden Rule—love your neighbor as yourself. Sometimes you can imagine that each of you has replaced your own part with that of your partner. It is as though your own hand's motions are echoed by the motions of your counterpart's hand. My hand moves slow and so does his. My hand moves fast and so does his. He grips hard, as do I. But it is better than doing it yourself. The feedback loop is not so small. It is not done so perfectly. You do not peak as fast. The results are not obtained instantaneously. You can ask another to slow down but if you say that to yourself you often won't heed your own command.

It is still a job, but one that is done by hand. Handcrafted.

Like something quaint from the Oneida Colonies, that 19th century communal group that practiced tantric sex, group marriage, and common ownership. If we examine a prime text like one of the versions of the *Joy of Gay Sex*, the emphasis is on anal intercourse. Even oral sex seems to be treated only as a part of foreplay. Everything is seen as leading towards the inevitable conclusion: butt-fucking. But let's face reality. That's not part of every date. Does it really matter by which method orgasm is achieved? The pleasure is all in your head and whether that release of bliss chemicals comes about through having your penis in an ass, a mouth or a hand, there is an orgasm. Perhaps not identical with one achieved with stimulation of the prostate, though that can be done manually as well. Could it not sometimes be better to have an orgasm without tooth-scrapes or skidmarks? Though a handjob can be despoiled by the displeasure of untrimmed nails or too-calloused, unlubed hands.

In Japan they sell sex toys for lonely men, rubber women's hands with painted nails that can be used as a masturbatory aid. It seems like a ghastly practice to use a severed hand for pleasure, a too-literal version of a fantasy. Yet why use that instead of a rubber vagina or the plastic "mouth" or "pussy" of an inflatable doll? Is the fantasy in the man's head of pleasure given by a woman too demure to offer the penetration of her orifices? Why shouldn't the man apply Nair to his own skin, paint his nails and imagine that his transvestite hand is that of his date? Some have suggested sitting on one's own hand until it grows numb and then masturbating with that, giving the feeling that the hand does not belong to oneself, or masturbating in front of a mirror thus turning a solitary act into a narcissistic circle jerk. Are there any porn stars famous for their handjob scenes? What is considered great handjob technique? Two-handed handjobs where one hand kneads the shaft and the other tickles the head, making the hand like a mouth? Giving Señor Wences-style handjobs with a lipsticked fist?

At one point in my life, mutual masturbation was the sex method I had experienced most often. Maybe it still holds the record; I've lost count. When I first masturbated, I lay in bed and imagined that my hands were a vagina. I put them together like a prayer. I had on several occasions previously rubbed my penis but only a few drops of precum emerged. I had not achieved orgasm but I knew what the natural process was and I tried to mimic it with my actions. It worked and my crotch was covered with warm goo of my own making. I had imagined that my hands were simulating a heterosexual act. I was so repressed I would not visualize my hands as the body part of a male, but rather of a female. It was a scientific thought. The sexual education my peers and I had received was predicated on the idea of us as young heterosexuals, destined to replicate the same sexuality as our parents. I can't imagine what it would be like to be a young person today in such a more overt world.

There was a rumor that a guy at my high school liked doing mutual masturbation with a girl. Michelle Tea once wrote that masturbating a guy was like changing a baby's diaper. Some women think jerking off a guy is like jerking off a dog. Somehow the act makes a guy passive. Her hand moves, the guy groans and maybe tosses his hips a bit. She manipulates him. He is manipulated.

There can be a feedback loop in the act. A lot of times I am the first to come and after, while still masturbating my partner, I am attuned to his pleasure and breathe as though I am going to come again although I am not. I feel his scrotum wrinkle to gauge where he is in arousal. I want to bring him to orgasm. That is my whole reason for being, as earlier it was his for me. To have and give that sublime pleasure. It's like a recipe that you've made many times before because you just love how it tastes. You never get tired of that meal so why should you tire of making love the same way sometimes? Sure, there are times when you want to try something new.

Handjobs are egalitarian. Everyone gets the same thing. It's like opening gifts on Christmas morning and finding you've bought each other the same thing. The first time I ever had sex with another guy, we did mutual masturbation. We were both in college and had roommates. We'd made out with our clothes on while lying on his bed and he'd humped me a bit but we'd never really gone all the way. We went up north to his parents' cabin. Cuddled a bit there. Then at their lake place we got fully naked. I shivered a lot, partially from the temperature but mostly from nervousness. His cock seemed a lot more compressed than mine, thinner but harder, like the same quantity of material in a smaller space, like Styrofoam with the air squeezed out. I jerked his cock and he jerked mine. He managed to come; I did not. After he'd gone to the shower, I jizzed alone just to prove to myself that I still could. Would I always be impotent with other men?

Do I really want to praise handjobs or am I just resigned to them? I admit that I like the pleasure of orgasm but while I am being masturbated I sometimes fantasize that other things are happening instead, like my dick is being sucked or I am fucking or that the finger in my ass is actually a cock.

The hand is nearly as nerve-rich as the officially recognized erogenous zones. Perhaps an unusually sensitive person could orgasm simply from the stimulation of rubbing against the palms. Maybe this is what can keep a person involved in the handjob even when his own genitals are not being stimulated.

I don't always love handjobs. Sometimes the job is just a chore. Sometimes when one of us has already come and would just as soon go wash up; the other's orgasm isn't in sight and the lube bottle is almost empty and the masturbator's forearm is cramping up and we both just sigh and apologize and that's it.

I have been stopped by AIDS prevention outreach workers on the street and asked to fill out questionnaires. There is usually a question about whether you use condoms during sex. Always, sometimes, never? There is no room on the form for an explanation of the kind of sex I usually have. There's no room to explain that I have one partner, no room to explain that we're sometimes not having penetrative sex in the sense of penis into mouth or anus. So I end up checking the same box as a barebacker, even though he's doing the most risky kind of sex and I'm doing the least risky. Or am I not even having sex by their definition? Should I just leave the question blank?

Is liking handjobs akin to having a mother who's a terrible cook but still craving her home cooking? What is the difference between good sex and bad sex? Good sex is supposed to mean you feel fulfilled. Maybe there's some thrill people get from transgressing societal taboos about penetration, but does that mean they're having better sex than me? When you've got your hands full of cock and your bird is in the other guy's hand, when you're beating out a polyrhythm on each other's drumsticks in the temperature of the interval of arousal, in the moment of fulfillment, that is when we fold our hands and give a prayer of thanks for mutual masturbation.

The Bear Majority

Statisticians tell us that most Americans are fat. Since gays are a subset of Americans, and we are consistently told that gays are no different from anyone else, it follows that the majority of gay Americans are fat. Therefore, most gay male Americans, issues of hairiness aside, could qualify as bears.

No doubt someone will try to refute this claim with anecdotal statements about gays being more likely to be gym members (but many gays are at the gym for cruising rather than fitness). However, evidence for my hypothesis can be found empirically. If you don't believe me, next June, stand on a corner as the Pride Parade crowd goes by and take an informal census. On the day when the most diverse cross-section of our community is visible in broad daylight, it will be clear that those with washboard abs are rare and those with love handles are plentiful.

But if bears are in the majority, bear images are not. The covers of gay magazines are plastered with muscle-bound, hairless young guys... and that's just the news magazines. Television also shows a narrow set of thin, white, young, urban, white-collar, able-bodied gay men, a representation which does not reflect reality. Some guys who don't claim the bear identity will resent being lumped in with the group. Regardless, twinks—the opposite of bears—are in the minority.

The media and advertising industry attempt to create an idealized gay figure that is presumed to be something everyone can identify with. It is assumed that not everyone could identify with a bear or, for that matter, with anyone besides a young, white Adonis. Some of the people in the media are allowing their own internalized self-loathing to block a more realistic portrayal of the true diversity of queers. Bears are an underserved majority. Rare are the safe sex posters or outreach materials produced by gay men's health organizations that feature bears.

Lesbians and straight women have done much more thinking, writing, and activism in the size acceptance movement. It's time for men to help hold up the banner. Bears could learn something by picking up on the work that's been done by women. Some bears may also be in denial about the need for size acceptance activism. While the bear movement has doubtless made some people's lives better, it has been somewhat disappointing in terms of creating awareness of its existence beyond a coterie, encouraging political awareness and engagement, or sparking societal change. Such ambitions are entirely appropriate and achievable.

Once a year, San Francisco hosts the International Bear Rendezvous, a time when the wider gay community finally "panders" to bears and welcomes their tourist dollars. While this weekend retreat may be fun and provide a chance to escape from rejection in the larger world, I'd like to encourage bears also to think politically and demand to be enfranchised. That may take the form of letter-writing, postering visibility campaigns, and engagement and solidarity with fat activists of all genders and sexualities.

Everyone's a Porn Star

People have the means of production of porn now more than ever. They can videotape themselves in broadcast quality. They can disseminate these images quickly and easily through the internet and, if they want, they can even be paid. One result has been the availability of a broader range of types of pornographic imagery. In the past, only someone with resources to produce commercial magazines or videos could disseminate their vision of what was sexually arousing. A limited number of people determined the answer to the question of what was sexy. There is plenty of crap. Endless badly posed and lit, amateurish images though sometimes the charm of amateurism is more arousing than the gloss of professionalism.

In my case, what I find arousing are images of clean-shaven fat guys. In the '80s when I was a teenager nothing was available. A decade after that, all that came close were the bear magazines featuring guys who were bulky but bearded. I like to be able to see a guy's face, to gaze upon his double chin and his chubby cheeks. Body fur I can take or leave.

Even the fat guy magazines like *Big Ad*, *Bulk Male*, and *Heavy Duty* mostly featured bears since that's apparently what the taste of the editors dictated. But now on the web I can find images of guys of every description easily. Many of them have the usual amateur problems: bad cropping, grainy images… but one of every hundred is decent and found arousing by me. Incidentally, most of those magazines were driven out of business after their images were scanned and distributed on the internet.

One could call it the democratization of porn, though it's a California-style democracy where everyone's a candidate but nobody is voting. Everyone can have porn and everyone can be in porn. There's something for everyone and presumably everyone is arousing to someone else. Or at least that hope remains. Formerly, pornographic models were simply the financially desperate but now the ranks have increased to include the sexually desperate. Everyone wants to be wanted. It used to be that many porn models were also prostitutes but now that everyone's a model, everyone's also a would-be whore. The bottom has dropped out of the market… or rather, there are more bottoms than ever, flooding the marketplace with free booty.

So many of these images are self-portraits that this could be seen as a kind of self-objectification. A person leaves out all the interesting details of their life and boils themselves down to a photograph (that probably doesn't resemble them strongly) and some likely inaccurate statistics. It's as bogus as a magazine playpal profile made up by a bored editor. People are afraid of appearing too interesting. It might frighten more people than it would attract to let it be known that you're both a Ph.D. *and* a porn model.

It makes for another twist in the child pornography dilemma when underage people are making images of themselves. There have been some prosecutions of these cases. But is it really better for kids to be looking at images of adults than images of each other? Is it exploitation if the kid is making self-portraits without coercion or profit motive?

It's inconceivable what being a kid today must be like with the ease of access to pornographic material.

Anyone who's looked at enough porn online has had the experience of spotting someone in real life whom you've seen sprawled naked in front of their webcam. It's a slightly jarring moment, sort of a celebrity sighting, a brush with infamy. It's hard to decide between asking for an autograph or a date. But it's also difficult to avoid feeling like a stalker, knowing so much information about someone. Maybe all those people wearing "Porn Star" t-shirts aren't lying.

Beyond Chubby-chaser

The focus of the queer movement has shifted back and forth between individual sexual fulfillment and improvement of life for a group in general. One gay subculture which coalesced in the 1970s was of chubby men and their admirers, known as chasers; the first social organization for these people was called Girth and Mirth. By analogy with the lesbian butch/femme culture, which also features a binary within homosexuality, and in order to acknowledge both elements, I refer to this as chubby/chaser culture. Later, that scene was eclipsed by the bear movement, which emphasized facial and body hair, and husky bodies. While these groups and their events have perhaps allowed people to get laid who would not have otherwise, Girth and Mirth and bear groups have been very apolitical. There has been some slight shift in mainstream gay culture, particularly in the acknowledgment of bears, though even bears have shifted to being "musclebears," bearded gym queens.

It would be nice if fat gay men could have the same chance as other gay men to have whatever sort of relationships they want. But many people automatically reject fat men. Fat gay men outnumber non-chubby men who will have sex with them, creating a situation where there is a stereotype that chasers are players who don't have to have any loyalty to a particular chubby man because they have plenty of other whales in the sea from which to choose. That doesn't mean that chasers hold all the cards. An attractive chub is still going to get more action than a homely chaser.

Sometimes I attend a monthly chubby dance night at a local San Francisco gay bar. The attendees complain about the music but there are no other alternatives catering to chubby men besides the bear bar. What about doing some other sort of event co-sponsored by the dance club which might provide other sorts of entertainment? For instance, a cabaret night that would allow for a variety of performances.

I envision a group which is not specifically a social group, but rather political. This political group would confront the supremacy of the gym body in mainstream gay culture: the compulsive use of photos of muscled gay men as illustration in gay periodicals; the lack of services provided by AIDS and safe sex information organizations targeting fat or bear men; the lack of acknowledgment of cultural and artistic production by fat and bear men. A side benefit of this political group would be incidental social interaction of like-minded gay men of various physical types.

Chubby/chaser culture—because of the visibility of fat men and invisibility of men who admire them—gives thin men the opportunity of remaining closeted and unpoliticized. Competition for thin men is a barrier to solidarity among fat men. A greater number of available fat men than chasers results in a disincentive for chasers to be monogamous.

In Marlon Riggs' classic gay African-American documentary, *Tongues Untied*, he puts forth the slogan "Black men loving black men is a revolutionary act." To swipe the concept: "Fat men loving fat men is a revolutionary act." People with this pattern of desire refer to themselves online as *chub4chub*. Everyone, fat men included, should consider fat men potential partners, and thin men should realize that not all fat men are interested in them.

There is a lack of theoretical and personal writing on and by fat gay males. There is much more writing by and about fat lesbians and straight women. Only recently have there been some books by and about bears. There have also been chapters on gay fat men in books such as *Looking Queer: Body Image and Identity in Lesbian, Bisexual, Gay and Transgender Communities* and *The Fat Studies Reader*.

When non-fat men are defined as "chasers," it limits us to the pursuit of fat men. I would like to suggest another possible identity, one pioneered by the fat women's movement, that of "fat ally": someone who shares a belief in resisting societal bigotry against fat people and works to help make improvements.

I feel comfortable around big men and enjoy the frisson of being around guys I find attractive even if we're not going to have sex. Sometimes I can meet someone who's interesting and friendly on top of being attractive. But it seems more likely to meet someone with shared interests at an event tailored to that interest, rather than at an event centered around a particular body type. The idea that people with bodies that are not the mainstream ideal have to make up for this with talent and personality doesn't always seem to hold true.

What really is the difference, except weight, between a circuit party and one of the big men's gatherings? A chance for an orgy, not for political planning that will make changes. Selfish pleasure, not working for the good of others. Call me moralistic, and perhaps prejudiced, since I haven't actually attended one of these events but I see no mention of formal discussion in the descriptions on websites, just eating, drinking, fucking, and minimal entertainment. Men should come together to critique the existing cultural representations and create new expressions based on their lives and bodies.

Other People's Kinks

Other people's kinks are funny. The name of my zine and website is *Holy Titclamps*. The very name is making fun of nipple-pinching S&Mers. Admit it, you've giggled at bizarre porn websites or gazed in shock at extreme body modifications.

Why are other people's kinks funny? Does it just mean we're hung up, guiltily giggling kids? Some things can be readily understood, while other kinks seem either too un-erotic or too painful to be pleasurable. Sometimes we recognize ourselves, but some unknown person has taken our mild preference to an extreme, bizarre end. On the Internet, people create websites where they shamelessly expose themselves and their predilections. We stare in disbelief that someone could be either that unashamed or that sociopathic.

It's not just erotic interests that people expose to ridicule. Nerds put up webpages about their interests of all kinds, those things they think are cool, and mean people make fun of them.

The laughter stops when it's your own kink that's the laughingstock, when your butt is the butt of the joke. It took you long enough to admit your fetish to yourself and finally enjoy it. Maybe your friends don't know about the twist that turns your crank. You've had to pretend to laugh along when they joked about your secret predilection (whether it's as general as homosexuality or something more particular like toe-sucking, or my own penchant, an attraction to fat guys).

Come on, folks, coming out is a never-ending process... your friends can deal with your kinks without treating you like the freak that you are or they're not really your friends. Go ahead and reveal your fantasies—who knows?—your friends may share them or may know a like-minded pervert they can introduce you to.

I imagine a coming out website where all the unashamed would appear under their real names, exposing naked pictures of themselves and lists of their kinks, all open to the world. Everyone in the world has had a nude picture taken, if only as a baby in the bath. It's a return to electronic Eden, where nobody wears a fig leaf anymore because nobody is ashamed.

Genital Branding

So you want your cock to look like it's been through some sort of primitive hazing ritual? So you want a sex organ that looks like it's been cooked in a waffle iron? You want a grid of scars on one of the most nerve-rich areas of the body? Give yourself pain in an organ built for pleasure? Okay, sicko, I'm sure you can find someone to help you achieve that goal.

An alternate take on "Genital Branding" is that it's a way of commodifying sex organs. The Penis 9000 Bio-Pleasure Organ. The Long John Silver. Penis of Delight. This cock will take you to the sun. Solar pleasure, organs of genital stimulation. The phallus as product.

Then you went into the dungeon chamber where the irons were sticking into a brazier of charcoal. Getting white hot. They were shaped at the end like cuneiform that would be stuck into wet clay to write the ancient Babylonian script... but instead of a cone of clay these words were to be written in your cylinder of flesh. Permanently... until death do your part in. You got yourself hard to be ready to take the burns. Your blood rushing into the organ of pleasure. Then the brander held your cock by its head and pressed the hot metal into your flesh. You scream, and the endorphins start to flow.

Everyone needs to buy a penis. It's on sale. $2.99. Loss leader. Own a piece of the rock hard penis. The penis is for sale. This is the brand of genitals that's most desired. You need to be a salesperson for the penis. You'll be on commission. The penis will take some sort of new incarnation. You'll be the salesperson of the penis. The penis is a brand. The Brand is a penis. The phallocentrism of capitalism. Penises are capitalist. Penises are commodified. You'll take the brand and create desire. The desire, not for sexual pleasure, but for possession.

After the first touch of the iron you thought you couldn't take it but after a dozen touches you're flying high on the pleasure drugs the brain makes to take us through pain. Your cock's on fire. There isn't anything you can do to turn back now. Each new burn mark cannot multiply the pain you feel. These burns are on the shaft, the head is left untouched. You will not be able to be stroked for weeks. Your cock will weep tears of pus from its burns. You will rub ointment into the burns and slowly it will heal. The wounds will be shiny and the marks will take you into a new level of respect. People will see you stride nude through the sex club, see the grid pattern of burns and wonder if that's really what it could be. Could someone be really that hardcore to have their penis burned with body art? Body artist. Collaboration between the brander and the human canvas. The ridges run down the shaft, and worshippers come to lick the scar tissue. They touch the art. There are no guards to keep them away from it. They worship your art, your cock. Genitally branded. Your face holds the key as well, brands on your cheeks and forehead. Beauty marks.

On every billboard in the land are giant images of scarred genital tissue, raised welts of burned flesh selling products, keratinous scars endorsing with the image of pleasure and pain. Buy this and you will have the experience vicariously without having your own flesh seared. Identify with the brand: genital brand identity.

Fashion Weak

Putting up with the way people look is one of the most unbearable burdens of being involved with subcultural scenes. For some reason, people find it necessary to adopt the most ridiculous forms of personal appearance. This is one of the worst aspects of alternative culture, exceeded only in annoyance by slamdancing and the glorification of drug use.

Let's start from the top. Nobody wants to see another bundle of white person dreadlocks or another eye-straining multicolor mullet dye-job. Faux-hawks should have been made illegal years ago. Facial hairstyles are even more farcical. Sideburns, soul patches, and even ironic moustaches will never change the world.

Nobody wants to look at your infected facial piercings. Stop fiddling with your tongue-stud... it's as "alternative" as an old man clacking his dentures. The distraction is too much to bear. Guess what? An eyebrow is not an erogenous zone, and there is nothing pleasurable about piercing them.

I wonder if there will ever be an explanation for the time spent hammering studs into the bills of caps or onto the hoods of sweatshirts. I muse about why one sees someone wearing a gray, holey t-shirt or moldy leather jacket advertising terrible taste in music. The craftiness of sewing silk-screened patches onto pants is to be admired... Li'l Abner would be proud.

The pain of tattoo application doesn't match the beauty of their bluish, faded, stretched-out reality. And if there's one thing stupider than a tattoo, it's a facial tattoo. Perhaps I should write "facial tattoos are dumb" on my forehead in magic marker and go to a punk show to make my point.

One hesitates to imagine the fungal foot infections concealed by the ratty Doc Martens or threadbare Chuck Taylors with which these masses are universally shod. Getting your toes stepped on by a platform Mary Jane clodhopper would make you agree that this fashion is not putting its best foot forward.

Now, I respect non-conformists but this is conformity, not its opposite. You only need to see a herd of these people in a nightclub or browse the bangs-in-eyes photos of an indie rock dating website to recognize the uniformity of these poses.

There is no correlation between how "alternative" someone looks and how alternative they actually are. Someone may have a mohawk and tons of piercings but be a mindless consumer, or someone may look completely normal yet be a politically active, culturally aware rebel. I guess the original point of adornment—including hair styling and coloring, jewelry, and dressing—was to make people look better. Perhaps in the case of these freak-styles, the point is to make people's appearance worse, in some sort of comment on looks-ist values.

Surely there must be some middle ground between the pathetic poles of designer labels on the one hand and crusty chic on the other. This is a plea for people to dress simply. A single badge or barrette should be enough to advertise that you are indeed one of the cool indie rock elite. Fashion victims of the world, undress.

Socially Responsible Pants

I need some socially responsible pants. I do not want to go to the Gap and buy a pair of pants sewn in a sweatshop in China and woven out of cotton grown with pesticides in a non-sustainable fashion. I need some good pants for those situations where I appear in public and don't want to look like the smelly countercultural type that I actually am; situations where I want to appear somewhat dapper and even professional, rather than sporting wrinkly old Dockers with an ink stain on the crotch and my undies showing through a rip. And you can't wear Guatemalan woven pants to an office. Every day is not Casual Day. My usual method is to let someone else absorb the bad karma for me. There are two approaches.

Perhaps one would buy pants secondhand. Secondhand purchase renders politically incorrect things (like fur, leather, and clothes made by slave labor) acceptable. Here's the life cycle of the pants: Biff, a cleancut young professional from the Marina district, goes to Old Navy and buys a pair of pants, ignoring the protesters outside. A couple of months later Biff decides the pants have been worn to slightly less than mint condition, or he stopped going to the gym and outgrew them, or he decided they had become marginally unfashionable. Rather than putting the pants directly in the trash, Biff at least has a shred of social conscience (perhaps embodied in the form of his wife and stroller-pusher, Jessica) and the pants, no longer of use to him, are donated to a charity. I go shopping at the thrift store, find Biff's pants, which are my right waist size and length and have a zippable zipper and no holes in the pockets. I buy them for about a fifth of what Biff paid for them. I wear them for a few years, only washing them after every four days of use, and wear a hole in the pocket from my keys, split the seam in the butt, shred the cuff with my bicycle chain, break the zipper, and finally tear a hole in the knee when I bend over to tie a shoe. The pants are shot, and no thrift store will take them. I look through the phone book trying to find a place that recycles cotton rags because I don't want to contribute to the landfill. Can you put raggedy pants in the green recycling bin to be composted? Maybe, but I'm sure my polyester blend sweatsocks with holes in them will not so easily degrade.

The other karma absorption technique is well known to college kids and middle class hipsters everywhere. Let your parents soak up the bad vibes. "Dude, I would so never buy these Nike Oppress-Airs, but bra, my mom gave them to me for my birthday." But since Christmas (which I don't believe in, but I'm not going to reject the gifts) is a long way away, I need to find some method of getting some not-only-socially-responsible-but socially-presentable pants.

I looked online, searching for "socially responsible" and "pants." I found a company that sells dress slacks made in Romania of sustainably grown organic hemp, sewn in non-sweatshop conditions (after all, the website notes, Romania recently became a member of the European Union, and they'll have none of that exploitation jazz). I got out my credit card, and almost clicked, but the pants are $82. They explain that the price reflects the cost of production since cotton is government subsidized and hemp is not. For that price I could get ten pairs of secondhand pants. See you at the thrift store.

Post-Style

"Do's and Don'ts" are both "Don'ts." I'm post-having-a-look, post-style. That means avoiding labels, haircare products, products in general, regimens, haircuts with names, piercings, etc.

What is the point of looking like a punk, like a hip-hopper, like a Chelsea boy, like a modern primitive? Apparently, to look like you're part of a group. I prefer to dress in a more neutral fashion, in a way that doesn't send any particular message, that doesn't alienate. There are people who will make assumptions about people if they're dressed in certain ways. That includes the people who dress in an out-of-the-ordinary way themselves.

The other day I was on my way home from seeing a band. There was a young guy with facial piercings and a blue mohawk twisted into dreadlocks. He had been at the same music show. He was talking to a woman on the bus about going to see a Sex Pistols reunion show and how Johnny Rotten was singling out individuals from the audience and putting them down for looking a particular way: for looking like what the stereotype of a punk is, in their mohawks and piercings.

What is the definition of a poseur? Someone who appears to be something they're not. But nobody is born a punk rocker, it's an identity that people take on. A poseur then is someone who has the look but in some way isn't punk rock. Is a poseur a punk you don't know yet? You don't know how much the person's exterior matches their interior. Hardly any other culture guards its gates so rigorously.

The longer I'm around, the less care I put into my appearance. I feel fine going out with greasy, uncombed hair, with food stains on my pants, with untrimmed nose hair. I don't care if I miss the attention of people who would judge me for such superficialities.

The people who end up on the "don't" list are trying just as hard as the people who end up on the "do" list. They just have worse judgment, or perhaps they are just too out of synch with the mainstream of fashion. I'm not going to end up on either list, because I've stopped trying.

Role Model

It's hard to be a role model: to be a preacher, a teacher, or a politician because you have to appear to be without blemish. Else your enemies will latch onto that weakness and drag you down in the mud even if it's not factual. If there's even a microgram of truth in the distorted allegations, a scandal may result. If people find the allegations believable, you may find yourself out of a job. If people are spoiling to get rid of you anyway, political intrigue may blow some slight indiscretion out of proportion and you'll find yourself in the gutter.

So it's necessary to hide your vices. These days, privacy is melting like a snowman. There's no way to be sure that someone isn't tapping your phone, reading your email, installing a spycam, or having moles in your organization. Paranoia can be a real timewaster.

If you're into getting stoned, having lots of sex with lots of people, looking at dirty pictures, getting drunk on a Friday night, receiving floggings or whatever turns your crank, it can be hard to give up that pleasure in the interests of your other passion, the life of a public figure. Especially a public figure supposedly the model of virtue.

Take me. I'm supposed to be a nice guy to everyone; someone in a long-term committed relationship with someone else everyone thinks is a nice guy. If any of that rings hollow I become some lousy hypocrite who's no longer everyone's favorite nice guy but just another example of an idol with clay feet. I'm also supposed to not have a big ego. But let's not kid ourselves, I want to be worshipped. Please do so. Money and gifts are gladly accepted.

It is known that I am an amateur pornographer in that I publish writing and art with sexual content. So far that information hasn't been used in any smear campaigns but perhaps indulgence in vice is now something to be emulated. My mediocre success (or perhaps it is mediocre failure) is not something on which people should pattern their lives. The role I am modeling is that of bohemian dilettante.

We have been given various flawed role models: addled celebrities, middling talents, people who prematurely decide that they have the answers despite lack of life experience. Their delusions of grandeur become public fodder through the work of publicists and hack journalists. Soon enough they are exposed as frauds while their personal and professional lives disintegrate. Perhaps the pressure of appearing as a public example contributed to the downfall.

The best role models are those who are unconscious of their role. Don't take a self-important person with an inflated sense of worth as an example of how to live. Nobody needs role supermodels, callow super-thin runway samples of how one is supposed to behave. Don't take your lead from the tabloids. Watch the people in your life you most admire.

An Open Letter to the Castro

Is this a neighborhood or a strip mall? Is there any common goal of liberation or only of turning a profit? Does anyone care about making this street a better place for everyone or only about making sure your property is worth more by the time you decide to sell and move to Palm Springs?

Why is there no longer a live performance venue in this area? Doesn't anyone have any vision of creativity or expression? Does anybody go to see live music performed, whether jazz, rock, or classical? Does anyone go to plays? Do people go to readings at the neighborhood bookstores? Or is all your time spent at the gym, drinking at a bar, or absorbing corporate entertainment?

I have a theory that the people who move to San Francisco are too afraid of non-conformity to come out fully in their hometowns. Instead, they can come here and be somewhat out without rocking the boat. They form a herd with other gay conformists.

I am alienated by the Castro. I don't have a gym body. I don't wear expensive clothes. I get snubbed as "uninteresting" by boring people. Smiling is forbidden in the Castro. Saying hello is taboo. Just having a conversation is unheard of. I try to put up flyers for my events and people rip them down. I wonder whether the poster-rippers ever participate in cultural events. Do they only destroy? Do they ever create?

There are gay publications that ignore live entertainment as a way to spend time. The only things they consider are those profitable events that pack men into a huge dance club after paying a high cover and dancing to loud music accompanied by moving lights. That's an embarrassingly unsophisticated way for an adult to spend time. I won't even call that mindless activity "hedonistic" because that implies that it's pleasurable. It isn't really pleasurable, it's just marketed to fool people into thinking that it is.

In New York or Chicago people will discuss their night out at the theater around the office water cooler. In San Francisco people don't realize that you're supposed to be sitting in a theater seat at 8 pm at night and go out to have a cocktail afterwards. The San Franciscan heads straight to the bar.

Drinking and doing drugs is the mark of someone who hasn't worked through the underlying reasons that they're self-medicating. You're supposed to have your life figured out and be over that stuff by the time you're in your 30s but San Franciscans are still out partying in their 50s, dressed in the clothes of their youth, failed Dorian Grays. It's a neighborhood of insanity at all levels of functioning. The crazy homeowners scream about the crazy homeless people. There is a certain tolerance for lunacy but the lunatics can't tolerate each other. The place seems like it should have potential as a place where gay people are concentrated.

Gay Real Estate

I'm a gay real estate agent and landlord. I've been making a killing by doing condo conversions in the Castro. Now I'm moving on to the Mission. It's looking like a real bargain and there's lots of great restaurants around here.

There are also a lot of dykes around here. It's a real hassle getting them out of their apartments. They don't just sit back and take it, they fight back.

There's one way that's easy to get to them: a lot of times, most of them aren't on the lease. There's a bunch of them living all in one apartment, like immigrants or something. But most of them aren't even on the lease, they're not supposed to be there. You know, original leaseholders move out, new ones move in. So you can just toss the new ones out, then the ones who are left don't have the money to make the rent. Easy as pie.

I was down at my Log Cabin Republican club the other day. At this point, there's no need for gays to be liberals; our interests are more in line with the Republican party. I get tips from my friends there on dealing with tenants. Tenancies-in-common, owner move-in evictions, Ellis Act... I know all the tricks.

I'm doing pretty well these days. I got in on the ground floor but I'm worried that some of these loopholes are going to close. My livelihood is being threatened by these so-called activists. I've been donating a lot of money to groups and politicians, and I think of it as an investment, one that I hope will pay off. These homeless kids coming to our neighborhood make me sick. They're just faking... they're not really gay, they're just trying to get a free lunch. Those bleeding heart types at the church want to shelter them, and we have to step on their needles and get panhandled by them. It's not like when I came to the city. Sure, I didn't have a job when I moved here. Yeah, I couch-surfed, but this is different. Don't ask me how, but it's different.

This city has a bright future. A lot of the bargains have been snatched up at this point so I'm looking a little further afield. Oakland is just ripe for the picking. I've even been looking into investments in Portland, I hear that's the next new hot town. So if you can afford to buy property in San Francisco, come by my office and let's deal. Otherwise, get out here!

New Gay Stereotype Jobs

Used to be all gay men were hairdressers, aerobics instructors, interior decorators, actors, waiters, and dancers. All lesbians were prison matrons, WACs, schoolteachers, and bouncers. Now there are new stereotype careers for homos.

Aides to politicians. Gay men are all about being polite and having manners, being verbal, and presentation. A perfect match for a politician's chief of staff or master of protocol. Did you hear about the "scandal" of Jesse Ventura's chief of staff exposing his own "staff" in a healthclub sauna? Unlike that misbehavior, many gays are good at sublimating their desires and channeling that energy into other areas—perfect for the manic pace of political campaigning.

Corporate Vice President of Sales. For the extremely driven lesbian, here's a position pressed right up against the glass ceiling, somewhere in the lower heights of management. The company can pat itself on the back for giving lipstick lip service to diversity. She's so driven that she has only time for career, not relationships, so the company doesn't have to feel guilty about not offering domestic partner benefits.

Computer programmer. Speaking of sublimation, for many late-blooming gays, their high school years saw their energy channeled into computers. The presumed asexuality of the geek provides a cover for those who want to remain closeted while the geek's freakiness and eccentricity makes it no surprise if the nerd comes out.

Social worker. Everyone knows homos are busybodies, always gossiping and prying into other people's business. Just like social workers. No wonder there is such an overlap in so many social workers and counselors are queer.

Garbage collector. For the butch fag, nothing is farther from the cologne-wearing stereotype than spending the day collecting trash. All that lifting eliminates the need to go to the gym. Just think of all the discarded porn collections waiting to be found in dumpsters. Imagine people's jealousy when your partner proudly tells his friends, "My boyfriend's a garbage man."

Career counselors are standing by to help you in your transition from an old-fashioned gay stereotype job to a new field like those mentioned here or others. It's time to do your colors and figure out what shade of the rainbow your parachute should be.

Imperial Rainbow

Balga-Fresno was a bucolic third world country. Life for people in the nation had never been too bad: the indigenous religion was not excessively moralistic and the missionaries who had evangelized the country had likewise been largely tolerant. The colonial period had involved only an average amount of oppression, and the post-colonial governments had not been exceptionally despotic. The country's major industry was a factory that manufactured items for personal use from the hardened sap tapped from an indigenous tree.

Because of the country's geographic isolation, news of the outside world was slow to filter in. Trends would be heard of as distant echoes and become the rage when they had long since become passé in first world countries. Frequently this would result in disappointment, as in the great Rubik's Cube craze of 1991, when a demand was created that could not be satisfied as the trendy item could no longer be imported because it could not be found.

One day, due to a shipping error, a crate full of a leading glossy gay magazine was mistakenly unloaded from a cargo plane. A curious post office employee, a tomboyish woman named Pandora, opened the abandoned crate. The magazines looked interesting so she took home a bundle of them and gave them to the members of her soccer team. Her cousin, Cupid, a graceful young man who was a student at the capital city's barber college, saw a copy of the magazine and demanded that Pandora bring some home for him to give to his fellow students. The effects of this random occurrence were like the chaotic hurricane instigated by the flicker of a butterfly's wing, for the women's soccer team was especially popular, and the students of the barber college could not help but discuss the contents of the magazine with their clients.

The articles did not make the biggest impression. The young people of Balga-Fresno were fluent in English (a language as easy to learn as it is grammatically consistent) and they easily recognized the handiwork of hack journalists. What impressed them were the ads featuring handsome, thin, white people. The people of Balga-Fresno, while handsome by their own standards, were by and large neither buff nor white. Due to the remoteness of their country, they had not developed an immunity to advertising and it devastated them like smallpox.

Their discontent with their lot in life boiled, and they marched en masse on the capitol demanding the importation of Miller Lite beer, the erection of an Ikea furniture store, and a shipment of light-duty pickup trucks for the women of the soccer team. Not since Stonewall has such a spontaneous eruption of gay rage against disenfranchisement graced the surface of this planet... but who would have guessed that the franchises demanded would be of this nature?

Balga-Fresno had come out of the closet and it wanted to buy gay freedom rings. In this case, because the trend of gay commercialism has not yet passed in our or any other country, their consumer demands *will* be satisfied.

Preserving Gay Culture

I have a new excuse for my consumerism: I'm preserving Gay Culture. Whether I'm purchasing a plaster cast of Michelangelo's David, the latest reprints of Gordon Merrick novels, gay porno magazines, designer clothes (designed by Gay designers, of course), or freedom rings, I am preserving for posterity the highest pinnacles of our glorious gay culture. This is not because I'm addicted to shopping or for my own benefit. I'm preserving these items for future generations of Gay people.

I am currently constructing (with the help of a multitude of willing slaves) a tomb which is to contain my mortal remains, carefully embalmed in the manner of the ancients, along with those possessions which will convey to some future archaeologist the Gay culture as it exists in the current dynasty.

Imagine, some thousand years hence, as some future Howard Carter breaks through the wall to find a dusty room crowded with the ephemera of my regal life. Enema bags, dildos, cockrings, pinky rings, nipple clamps, cone bras, wigs, posing pouches, all gilded and bejeweled with faience and lapis. My pet cats mummified (as I am so often tempted when my furry little children misbehave!) and a treasure trove of Gay Culture.

After all, we are the ones who harbor the pinnacle of Western culture. Visit your local mega-record store (if one still exists where you reside) and enter through the soundproofed doors to the classical music section. You will find nobody there but Gay men. Sure, there are plenty of Gay Philistines shopping for techno out in the rest of the store but, in this section, one finds the true elite of the Gay world, the crème de la crème. Similarly, who visits art galleries? Heterosexuals only know to visit museums when "must-see" shows are hyped. Let's face it, the muses are fag-hags, and Parnassus is a cruising-ground.

When I buy, I am not simply propping up capitalism, participating in a system in which elites buy luxuries while the poor do without. No, I am building a new Alexandria, an empire whose glory will be in dust.

Dirty Nails, Hair and Body

Welcome to Dirty Nails, Hair, and Body, a new salon for men. Are you tired of people seeing your hands and immediately clocking you as a pampered white collar worker? We'll work your nails until they're cracked and worn. We'll rough up the edges to make them look bitten enough to give Samuel Delany a woody. And with a trademark secret bonding technique, we can give you calluses. We can give you hands that look like a honest workingman's hands without the honesty or the work.

Also, try out our sun salon! Just put on a wife-beater t-shirt and lie down on a bed with all the sun's unhealthy glow to build up a good farmer's tan, redneck's burn, or lop-sided trucker blush. Get a caustic facial and derma-over-abrasion to bring out the spider veins in your nose and cheeks and give you the ruddy complexion of a hard-drinking dockworker. Charles Bukowski popularized acne-pocked cheeks, and now you can have the look, too. We even can arrange with a doctor to give collagen injections for a Karl Malden nose or the jowls of experience. Referrals are available to a plastic surgery specialist who can do lipojection to give you a good beer belly without the effort of drinking all that beer.

Our hairdressers are accomplished at many styles, from mullets to accentuating receding hairlines. We have the lotions to give your hair that authentic barfly grease-sheen. Forget daily regimens of repeated shampoos and conditioning. Just run a black plastic comb across your dandruff-flaked scalp and you're ready to go.

We even have a fragrance counter with a line of manly musks and breath enhancers. Smell this sampler and witness the notes… a whiff of cigarette ash, a swig of whiskey, hair of dog, eye of newt, and a soupçon of smegma. After a visit to our salon, the boys will be squealing to each other, "Ooh child, who is that sexy dirty old man?"

What is authenticity, anyway?

Queer Kids Catalog

Kids these days are coming out younger and younger. When I came out, I was 19 and in college. At the time, my college didn't have a gay student group, I had to go to the other more liberal college in town to find a coming-out group (and boyfriends). Since then, even the high school I went to has started a gay student group. What's the next illogical step: elementary school coming-out groups?

And with grade-school age queers, it means yet another marketing opportunity: Toys "R" Us meets Queer Nation. Another business opportunity for *Larry-bob's Lifestyle Catalog*.

Spandex gym outfits in kids' sizes will allow gym queens in training to have outfits as hideous as their adult counterpoints. Bizarre clothing cuts and eyeball-wrenching color schemes will help ease the transition from gym class bully target to future bodybuilding champ.

Junior-size weights will allow young lifters to train so by the time they're of age their chests and abs will be developed enough to not face rejection. Sure, weight-lifting by children can result in problems with bone development but them's the breaks.

Candy poppers will serve as a sugar-coated gateway to future drug use. Packaged in a little vial that looks like video head cleaner, this item is sure to spark controversy.

The kids these days are all into video-games so we carry a line of queer-themed vids. Vicarious criminal activity like shooting and stealing automobiles, and virtual housekeeping simulations… now with a rainbow color scheme.

Junior bondage kits so you don't have to rely on tying your partner to the swingset with a jumprope anymore. You'll no longer need to use the toy handcuffs from your old detective kit. Talk about kid leather! Youth-sized t-shirts with gay slogans like "Grade School Lesbian" and "Future Fister." Nothing's shocking anymore.

Our offerings are like gay training wheels so that kids can move smoothly from "questioning" to "gay consumer" with nary a spill.

How to be an Annoying Gay Couple

We're an annoying gay couple. We're getting this off on the right foot. It's important to use the right pronoun. It's WE. We don't have opinions of our own as individuals. We agree on everything. We have the exact same taste in campy movies, in interior decoration, in small barky dogs, in gardening, in feng shui, in tasteful gay erotica photo books (though oddly, neither of us lives up to the beauty standards in the books).

We're an annoying gay couple. We've been together for over a dozen years. Every time we give ourselves an opportunity to brag about long we've been a couple, people are very amazed and coo. We're not too modest to act proud about an accomplishment which is simply the result of inertia and laziness. We're the very picture of gay bourgeoisie. We reside in a duplex and live off the rent we exorbitantly charge to our downstairs neighbors whose every peep we complain about as if they were staging Altamont in their living room.

We make pains to always be seen in public together. We're inseparable. Joined at the hip and all those clichés. We have pictures of us together hugging inanely in matching sweaters on our desks at work. Every room in our house has framed photos of us on our vacations in exotic locations. We commissioned a photo-realistic acrylic painting of ourselves that hangs in pride of place in our living room. Images of us are also reproduced on coffee cups and matching cross-stitched seat covers which our mothers made.

Our families are very accepting of our relationship, at least to our faces. Behind our backs, they find us tedious and neurotically annoying. Our friends, gay and straight, have a similar public and private reaction. We dote on our pets, and it's a good thing we don't have actual children who would be even more annoying in public than the children of the average heterosexual couple. They'd be awful spoiled brats in embarrassing designer clothes, like living porcelain dolls.

Our role models are Rosie and Kelli, Phyllis and Del, Harry and John, Christopher and Don, Lily and Jane, Elton and what's-his-name that did the documentary about him, Gertrude and Alice, Orton and Halliwell, Paul and Jane, Oscar and Bosie, Merchant and Ivory. But we'll never have a messy public breakup like Lance and Reichen, Ellen and Anne, or other couples that made the mistake of going public with their relationships too early. We're too co-dependent ever to break up. We plan on having a murder-suicide pact should anything ever go drastically wrong.

We don't have any secrets from each other because our lives are too boring to have any secrets. We spend every waking moment when we're not at work in close proximity to each other. We never argue in public. For all people know, we never argue, period. We never talk to friends about any problems that might exist within the relationship so, for all people know, our relationship is absolutely blemish-free.

Every one of our slutty friends says that he wishes he could find the perfect man like we have found but he's never willing to put any energy into an actual relationship. He's psychologically fucked-up and a pretty much complete mess, something he seems to be unaware of. He always blames the other person. But we are completely psychically whole. Somehow, without the aid of therapy, we have managed to have perfect lives and a perfect relationship. Nothing could be wrong.

We don't talk about our sex life in public, and of course nobody would be rude enough to inquire into it. We don't know what people say about us behind our backs. Perhaps they think we're neurotic queens who are obviously both undersexed bottoms sublimating their sexual desires into home maintenance... but I doubt it. They probably suspect the truth, which is that we have spiritual, intense, mutually-satisfying, aerobic sex on a much more frequent basis than those desperate individuals who must arrange their sexual assignations on a one-by-one basis, living sexually hand-to-mouth, never knowing where their next meal is coming from.

People have a love-hate relationship with us. We're what they hope for, yet we also embody the self-loathing that they feel as homosexuals. We're the best they could ever be, but that's still not that great. Is this all there is to aspire to? To have a white picket fence, pets, house, cars, jobs, a DVD collection? Surely there is some higher purpose in life. Even singing off the same part in the Gay Men's Chorus doesn't really speak to spiritual fulfillment. Our pinnacle seems barren. Our relationship still isn't as valuable as a heterosexual relationship. We've had a commitment ceremony, which was certainly one of the most annoying things we've ever done. We worked out vows with a spiritual practitioner. We dressed in lavender tuxedos. We had the most artistic flower arrangements ever. We got married in a garden. We had vegetarian food at the reception. Our biological families attended, even a cousin or two. But people don't give the same caliber of gifts to gay couples.

When we're on vacation, it's immediately obvious to everyone that we're a gay couple. We hold hands, even in Islamic countries. We consult each other on every knickknack we pick up in European flea markets. We always ask at bed and breakfasts whether we can get a queen-size bed, but they're rarely able to comply. It's not like we're actually going to have sex since our shopping expeditions invariably have left us too exhausted to consummate our relationship.

Every few months we affirm our commitment by flying to whatever country or city has most recently legalized gay marriage and get re-married in a shower of rice and bouquets. We have a completely equitable partnership. Everything is shared. We don't have any possessions which we consider "his" or "mine." We even use the same toothbrush. Fortunately, we wear the same size clothing. Sometimes one of us looks in the mirror and gets a start, thinking the image is that of the other one. We have no fixed rules about who is the chef, who is the gardener, who is the mechanic. There is no division of labor. We are both equally skilled in everything but we complement each other nonetheless, paradoxically.

We've Photoshopped pictures of ourselves as children together, creating a false history that we knew each other even before we met.

Check out our interminable website full of photographs of us and our pets. We have dinner parties with other annoying gay couples. We like to cook elaborate multi-course meals. Our relationship is better than those of these other couples. We can tell that there's a note of hysteria in their closeness, cracks in the public image, a veneer of respectability over a morass of infidelity, dishonesty, and compulsive behavior.

There's the matter of what to call our relationship. Life partners: makes you want to knock on wood. Boyfriends: too immature. Lovers: too ishy and '70s. Husbands: too assimilationist (if that's possible). No word has the perfection to match the perfection of our relationship.

I ask the homophobic religious right: you say that homosexuals are promiscuous? But what about our loving relationship? We're putting the lie to the truths you tell. But there are millions of other homosexuals who are promiscuous, and just because we're virtuous in our sin, doesn't make us any better than them. Everyone deserves to have equality but some animals are more equal than others.

If we had coffee with Jesse Helms or Pat Robertson, I'm sure they'd be very charmed by our pleasant personalities and the delightful way we've decorated our home. Their wives would probably want the recipes for the fantastic meals we made, and we'd also beat them at arm-wrestling thanks to our workouts... at the gym we spot each other.

We're lovers, friends, ride a tandem bike, paddle double-holed kayaks, and rappel each other down cliffs. We do aikido and contact improv dance together. Anything that two fellas can do together, we do together, like a film montage of fun. Our role models are *Thelma and Louise*, Leopold and Loeb, Genet's *Maids*, Verlaine and Rimbaud, those Australian mother-killing girls, *Butch Cassidy and the Sundance Kid*... outlaws who annoyed you because they were dangerous and would fuck you up. Scary homos. Lipstick and switchblades. Super creeps. We take pleasure in rejecting people who hit on us (though it only happens every couple of years.) Three-ways, swingers, open relationships... Horrors! We're much more evolved than that. But we don't have any reason for jealousy. We don't desire anything else. We're like a pair of swans. Mated for life. Sadly, that's how we each felt with our last boyfriends, but I guess they didn't feel the same way. Our role models are Zeus and Ganymede, Alexander and Bucephalus (or was that his horse?), Hercules and Iolas, Xena and Gabrielle, David and Jonathan, Gilgamesh and what's-his-name.

We are role models for the gay world of modern times. Our life together will somehow be an example that people will base their existences upon. But how we achieved this perfection is a mystery. People ask us for advice and we have little to give. We don't know how to explain how this beautiful relationship came to appear. Are we just naturally nice guys who could get along with anyone? Does anybody have the potential to achieve this kind of relationship or are some people too damaged, too unbalanced, too neurotic, too individual to live a long-term successful couple relationship like we do?

We don't crave acceptance. All we ask for is tolerance. Because tolerance is all that most people can manage when they have to put up with an annoying gay couple.

Mary, Mary, Quite Contrary

I am a contrarian. Since childhood, I have done stuff simply because it's not what others were doing. I don't appreciate sports. I have never been an alcohol drinker (sure, I've had a sip or two but I've certainly never been drunk). I've never smoked a cigarette. I've never toked pot or used other mind-altering substances. I'm a vegetarian. I'm a homosexual.

I suppose I could carry it further and refuse to drive a car, adjust to a full vegan diet, and stick my middle finger up at the government by becoming a tax resister. But I haven't reached that point yet. Once enough of the things I do that were extraordinary have become rote, perhaps I will have to expand the borders.

Even when I do things that are out of the ordinary, I do them differently than other people. For instance, I am not an average gay. I have had long hair when most homosexuals have had short hair. I listen to indie rock when most of them are dancing to house music.

People ask me frequently why I'm a vegetarian, why I don't use mind-altering chemicals. I say I live this way for no reason—therefore anyone can. I have altered more minds by *not* smoking marijuana than

I could have by passing a joint to a room full of people.

It could be said that I'm appropriating the tradition of the backwards "contraries" of Native American societies who did everything in reverse, holy fools.Rebellion is assumed to be childish, which must mean that conformity is a sign of maturity, which seems like a ridiculous position. I disagree with saying conformity is best, a phenomenon which has resulted in little good. It is a harbinger of stagnation, of lack of insight and fresh ideas. While being contrary may be seen as childish, it may also be seen as wise, as standing for moral choice rather than settling for general assumptions of what is acceptable behavior.

The Mess Manifesto

I am a homosexual slob and I'm proud of it. I am a rebel against the stereotype of the tasteful and fastidious fag. That prissy homo is: valence curtains, statue of David, faux-finish sponge-painted walls, recessed lighting, wall sconces, Persian carpets, Nagel prints, uncluttered surfaces, wood floors.

I am: papers everywhere, thrift store sofa, toys on the mantel, dirty clothes on the floor, unmade bed, cat hair in the corners, unmopped floor, plaid curtains, dirty dishes, soap scum shower, unflushed toilet, overflowing litterbox. I am a filthy homosexual. And I like it that way. When I see an immaculate fag home I wonder, Where are the papers? Where are the books stacked sky-high? Where is life taking place on this bare lunar surface of a dwelling space? They themselves have no interiors, their beings are as uncluttered as the interior decors of their houses. House beautiful, soul void.

And I'm subverting the expectation of homosexual tastefulness. What purpose is this signal that one has taste? That one knows how to decorate, surround with beauty? Oasis in a world of ugliness. But that isn't an ugly world: there is beauty in its squalor. My place is not cluttered or squalid enough yet; I see the chaos of a junkyard as inspiration.

You get stuff done when your materials are at hand. Obviously these people don't get stuff done. They don't do zines (or their houses would be a firetrap of papers), they don't make music (that would result in electronic cables everywhere or piles of music books), they don't paint (now there's a messy pursuit). Instead, they spend their time dusting the mini-blinds. There are precedents, such as Quentin Crisp, who once said that after the first couple years of not cleaning the dust doesn't get any worse.   O horrid creatures that devote themselves to housework rather than the creation of great art! For what purpose do they think they were placed on this earth? Certainly not to keep it free of dust. What inspector will ever arrive to run a finger across their mantelpiece and declare it immaculate? What inspector, whose opinion truly matters? When the time comes to fling open the chest that ought to be filled with manuscripts, it will be bare. All the housecleaning in the world will turn to dust the week after you pass on to another plane but if you create art, it shall live forever.

It's not too late if you're one of those neatniks. Every time you feel the urge to clean, sit down and write something, open a sketchbook, sit down at the piano. In a matter of weeks, you'll not only have some artistic production to show, your home will be well on the way to being a proper bohemian sty.

Rethinking the Mess Manifesto

I have been reading my *Mess Manifesto* at open mikes. While it gets a good response and I hear from people who are even bigger slobs than me, I wonder if maybe I've gone too far. I still think I'm correct that creating things that last is what's important. My credo is still "The Meaning of Life is the Creation of Art." It's also true that disorganization can get in the way of being creative. If I can't find the book I want to refer to in an article, if I can't find the CD it's time for me to review, if I don't have a quote from someone because I procrastinated too long about asking them... then my mess is getting in the way of my art.

And I waste time. Time that could be used—if not directly for art-making—at least for getting organized. Searching through the boxes of papers that fill my living working room can take time. I try to follow a maxim of "Sort, don't search." When something is missing, rather than dig through piles of stuff to find it (which may only add to future disorganization), I try to sort through things so that I'm more organized in the future. Often I find what I'm looking for and (as a bonus) things that I've been unable to find in earlier search missions.

I am to the point where I can't have people visit in the apartment because there is too much crap. I have a social life in cafes. I can't reciprocate when people invite me to their homes for dinner. I barely cook anymore and even though the kitchen utensils have been simplified to the point of having only one plate and fork per person, there are still unwashed dishes in the sink.

When you publish a zine for over a dozen years, a zine that has included reviewing every other queer publication that existed, and when you don't sort that stuff as it comes in and you never throw anything away, you end up with a huge backlog of stuff that's jamming things up. I recently heard the advice that it's best to start with the current stuff you're working with rather than going through old stuff since today's mail is tomorrow's boxes full of crap. I have deferred deciding on what to do with my papers for so long that getting organized seems to be impossible.

What I have is not to be thrown away. There are publications that I possess that nobody else does (but I don't know if I can find them). There was a time when I alphabetized zines but that was a decade ago. Now even those boxes are on shelves in the back of a closet packed past waist high with collapsing cardboard boxes.

I went to my day job on a Sunday and spent six hours throwing away and sorting. At least that area of my life is fairly organized (until the next time my cubicle becomes an outpost of Grey Gardens). It's hard to escape the distractions of the computer at home enough to get the real world organized. I know that renting a storage space is not the solution. This is an area where I know there is a problem but I do not yet know what the solution is.

VII. Nature vs. Nurture

Childhood Conditioning

What if we turned out like we did because of how other kids treated us? Kids who got called "fag" turned into faggots. Kids who got called "fatso" ate and got fat. Those who got called "brain" got smart. Those who got called "stupid" are now failures. I wonder when I was first called "faggot." Probably some time in junior high school—there was a number of guys who would taunt and punch me. There was a time when I didn't know what the word "fag" meant. I thought it was a verb, a synonym for "fuck." People would say stuff like "those two are gay together."

When I was in elementary school, there was a gay rights law overturned in St. Paul and other kids said that I was at City Hall protesting. I hadn't been but I was a second generation liberal with a vague idea that this was a social justice issue. I hadn't personalized it. But maybe those kids saying that planted the idea in my head that that is where I belonged.

When I was in junior high, I would write obscene doggerel poems teasing my friends and they would do the same back. I did one where I said my friend Christopher, who was being raised by a single dad and had been born in the San Francisco area, was named after Christopher Street. I have no idea how I'd heard about Christopher Street. The poem made him really mad, though, and he turned it in to a teacher who was going to make me take it home to my parents but I intentionally lost it. I talked to them about it but didn't spell out exactly what I had written and they said that maybe it made Christopher mad because it was true.

One time, probably during junior high when I went to the Renaissance Faire with my piano teacher and his friends (all presumably gay), one of them commented that I was like a little adult. "Adult homo" could have been implied. I guess they had some recognition of who I would probably grow into. Another time, after I'd turned pages for my teacher at a piano recital we went over to his friend's condo. The guy had a collection of Japanese ivory carvings—netsuke—which I thought were interesting. I had the impression the guy was divorced. My piano teacher had at one point been the roommate of our church organist and he had another roommate now: a thin, balding man with an anchor tattooed on his arm from a stint in the Navy.

There was just sort of this vague cultural awareness of homosexuality. The Village People, rumors of David Bowie, local whispers about an intergenerational sex scandal at the Children's Theatre Company. My mother knew a woman whose son went to the Children's Theatre school—at one point he acted in a production of Pinocchio, and also in an original production about a wizard. Later he was one of the kids involved in the scandal when it came to light; subsequently, the director was banned from contact with youth.

I got haircuts at a place where the haircutters were a couple of queeny guys. One of them was a Southerner named Farrel who had a clone mustache. I even wrote about them in my diary as a possible character study for my writing. Did they recognize my nature, about which I was in denial? It all just seemed part of general 1970s flamboyance: Flip Wilson in a dress, Doug Henning's rainbow hippie magician clothes, Robin Williams' suspenders. All the things kids said about homosexuality were just teasing and innuendo. I remember talking on the school bus, speculating about whether a certain male gym teacher was gay. Nobody would actually identify this way… until that flamer Danny in high school, whom I avoided.

Why didn't I ever ask myself what it was that made adults want to get married or have lovers? Adults had some mysterious other thing that made them want to do things that kids didn't do. Nobody offered me an identity other than heterosexual.

Little fuzzy baby animals grow into ferocious adults. We'd go to the zoo and look into the dark at the humping binturongs in the nocturnal exhibit. My uncle castrated a calf at a neighbor's farm. I didn't learn much from nature, though. Just a few short years later I was a punk and then gay, too, before the end of the '80s. I guess the conditioning took.

Changing Your Name

Almost the first thing that happened after you were born was that your parents named you. You got stuck for your whole life with some appellation that was chosen for you before you were formed. I have a theory that people are, in part, shaped by their names. People stereotype you by your name and they'll treat you with expectations formed by other people with the same moniker as you. So you'll grow into being someone who is typical of people with that name. This is especially true of people with unusual names. There's automatically something about you that doesn't fit in. You're already othered.

Some people get sick of the name their parents gave them so they change it. It's pretentious to name yourself—it's always fortunate when friends come up with a nickname. I was given the name Larry-bob: a friend figured out that if he contracted my given first and last names that would be the result. When I started doing a zine, I adopted that as my penname.

Some punks change their names to scary-sounding Viking warrior shit, or they have their band or zine as their last name. Kind of like how people used to get the name Smith or Miller based on their vocation. Will there be future generations of people named Cometbus? Should I legally change my name to Larry-bob Holy Titclamps?

Changing your name is almost a joke but it means you're controlling maybe the only thing you can, like piercing or tattooing which is done on the thing you firmly own on earth, your body. It's self-expression. Using an assumed name is not the same thing as being anonymous. I have two decades of reputation tied to the name Larry-bob. Besides which, I've always included my real name in my zines. I'm not anonymous when so many people know me as Larry-bob.

There are some people whose real names are almost secret. It's a delight to discover that Jello Biafra was born Eric Boucher, or that Medea Benjamin was first named Susie. Typically, though, even when someone has changed their name, her parents will call her by the name they initially gave, or even more humiliatingly, by a childhood diminutive. It's amusing to phone when someone is visiting their parents and hear someone's mother call for "Paulie" or some such embarrassing appellation. You can sometimes tell at what age people met someone by what name they call them, especially when the person has gone by as many different names as a tree has rings.

Calling people by their preferred names means you're following the rules they set. Calling people by some past name could result in various responses: from signaling closeness and history, to cruelly bringing up a past era preferred forgotten, to disrespectfully ignoring a new gender. On the other hand, some people return to using their original names. In some cases, this is related to the desire to reclaim family connections that had at some point been estranged.

If you haven't yet changed your name, what's holding you back? Do you really want to spend the rest of your life as a Herman Brown when you could be a Rainbow Starspackle Laughingchild?

1978

1978 was a year of amazing activity in the realm of gay politics. In January, Harvey Milk, who had been elected a couple months previously, was inaugurated as a Supervisor in San Francisco. That year he fought the Briggs Initiative, a California ballot measure that would have banned gay teachers. In November 1978, the Briggs Initiative was defeated. Later that month, Harvey Milk was assassinated.

In 1978 I was eleven going on twelve and living in St. Paul, Minnesota. I was not precocious and self-aware of my sexuality but I already had a sense of social justice. St. Paul had a gay rights ordinance, initially passed in 1974, though I doubt I was aware of the law before Anita Bryant-inspired conservatives made efforts to repeal it. I certainly knew about it when they did though.

I remember standing on the playground steps of the St. Paul elementary school, Webster Magnet, where I was in sixth grade when one of the other kids teased me, claiming that on TV footage of gay rights advocates protesting the repeal of the ordinance, he'd seen that I'd been there. I hadn't and I denied it. I didn't have awareness then of how my sexuality would be expressed but I understood that this repeal represented an injustice to gay people. In fact, the kid teasing me was being raised by a single mom who I knew was as liberal as my parents and no doubt she opposed the repeal as well.

My parents and I attended a liberal church, one that was part of the United Church of Christ (formerly Congregational) and Presbyterian denominations. Since that time, the congregation has voted to declare itself "Open and Accepting" and a "More Light" congregation, both signs of acceptance of gays. At the time, however, there was some controversy. A seminary student interning at the church, the organist, and the youth choir director had composed a letter opposing the recall. They may have even printed it on church stationary. They were reprimanded for this action. The organist is still with the congregation and now is openly gay. The church even had the writing of gay-supportive hymns as a theme for its annual hymn-writing contest. But back in 1978, the bigots got their way and the ordinance was repealed.

I don't recall having much awareness of Milk and San Francisco mayor George Moscone's assassinations or subsequent events, such as Dan White's trial and the White Night riots. The same month in 1978 as the Milk-Moscone killings, the mass suicide in Jonestown did register with me as a news event. A couple years went by, and in 1980 my parents and I spent six months in Berkeley, California. At my junior high school health class, guest speakers came to class: a gay man and a lesbian. The man was Blackberri and he was the first gay man I'd heard speak openly about his life. (He is known for his music and his appearance in a couple of gay documentaries, *Word is Out* and *Tongues Untied*.) I don't remember the teacher's name but in retrospect he probably was a gay man. If the Briggs Initiative had passed in 1978 he would not have been able to bring these speakers to class since that would have been considered advocating for gays, something prohibited by the initiative.

I didn't really learn about Harvey Milk until the education which was part of my coming out while attending St. Olaf college when I absorbed gay culture in a flurry of reading, watching documentaries and dramatic movies, and participating in social activities with the gay and lesbian students of Carleton, the other, more liberal college in Northfield, Minnesota.

Finally, to fast forward a few years, in the Fall of 1991, as I was preparing to move from Minnesota to San Francisco, St. Paul finally had a new gay civil rights ordinance and the time came to confirm it at the ballot box, as the expected initiative challenge had arisen. I volunteered to make phone calls urging people to vote. This time, the voters supported gay rights. It had taken over a decade to come to this point. The kid who had been teased on the playground had grown up and was now able to speak for himself.

A Red Crayola is a Good Substitute for a Penis

I was about seven years old when Wendy confronted me. We were by the bathroom at the private Montessori school we attended. She was a little younger than me. She had a thin, pointed, paper-wrapped, brick red crayon stuck in the fat folds of her naked girl cunt. She said, "Look, I've got one too."

How Freudian can you get? Her penis envy, my castration fear of the loss of my penis. It's some sort of classic text.

She told me, "Look, I've got one too," so I would look and see her penis. My penis was in my pants, invisible. She had a penis and I did not. I was a good boy, she was a sexual girl-boy. I was effeminate because I behaved. She was masculine because she acted out. I passively said nothing in my discomfort and walked away. I told a teacher what had happened and Wendy was reprimanded, but that is only a vague recollection, not something as visually imprinted as the moment of confrontation.

She was an only child. She could have wanted to be her businessman father's son. A younger brother yet to come could have replaced her as his favorite child. I had a brother myself but no sister. I had not seen a girl naked below the waist before, only the fuzzy furry crotch of my mother as she changed into a swimsuit, somehow vaguer than my father's impressive penis. These were terms my parents used, the scientific ones: penis, vagina, bowel movement.

I can still picture the beige wall tiles of the bathroom, the pulled down stretchy snagged tights Wendy wore, the plaid of her hiked up skirt, the black of her patent leather shoes. She was dressed by her parents in a traditionally feminine way, her hair at a bobbed length, a 1970s version of Shirley Temple, but perhaps given her own choice she would have wanted to appear as a tomboy.

The incident frightened me because it was outside the realm of my experience. I did not experience it as an invitation to play along or to examine more closely, and I never had that sort of sexual play with another child. I do not recall specifics of being instructed about correct behavior for public nudity. Sculptures of nude children by Vigeland which I saw in Norway's Frogner Park and again in the snapshots my parents had taken of them made an impression on me. Our photo albums also included nude photographs of me as a baby being bathed in a sink. There was another one of me at about age three naked and standing, laughing, one leg raised and bent at the knee and with a hand raised, palm towards the viewer. Caught in a gap between two pieces of furniture as though playfully chased and then captured by the camera's shutter. But I would never have exposed myself as Wendy did. Even in later years, I was shy about public changing rooms.

This was not the last trauma that she brought into my life: a year or so later she hit me in the head with a baseball bat as I walked in front of home plate. I suppose that the bat is yet another phallic symbol while the irregular pentagon of home plate is like a stylized pictogram of the female genital area and the injury to my head represents castration. We related to each other like some sort of psychologically fraught *Peanuts* comic. She sought my attention and I rejected it. I feared her wild strange power. Her name also suggests the story of Peter Pan, a narrative with which I was familiar as a child. A girl flies away with the lost boys. But this Wendy had none of the surrogate mother qualities of her fictional namesake.

In the bathtub I would push my penis back into my body with my finger, pull the scrotum up over it until I was as smooth as her crotch. Or hiding my penis between my legs, look at myself in the mirror. The anxiety of potential loss can be lessened through play.

Where and how is Wendy today? Has the frilly girl become William? Or does she maintain a female identity but still pack something extra? Perhaps her narrative became ordinary vanilla heterosexuality, while her childhood deviancy affected my adult life. I find myself surrounded with boys who were once girls, girls who were once boys. I still cling frantically to the gender identity which I was assigned at birth, ignoring the possibilities first offered by a girl with a red Crayola penis.

I Hate Sports

I hate sports but I end up financially supporting sports because my taxes pay for stadiums. When I buy a newspaper, I end up with a useless waste of trees called the sports section. The TV shows I enjoy are pre-empted by baseball games in extra innings. When I'm at the laundromat, a television blares out a big game. It's moronic: adults watching absurdly overpaid adults playing a child's game.

I don't attribute my lack of interest in sports to my sexuality. There are plenty of gay men who are into sports, and even more lesbians who are as well. Maybe getting whacked in the head with a bat during that playground game of baseball turned me against sports.

I had plenty of other bad sports experiences growing up. Physical Education is a contradiction in terms. The coaches don't teach people the rules but rather assume that people already know everything about the all-American games of football and baseball, but I never thought to complain. It seemed to be cross-cultural. When I went to school in Norway for three months in fourth grade, the gym teacher didn't explain the rules of Cricket (maybe because he couldn't express himself in English) and I ended up skipping gym class.

Gym teachers play favorites and seem to prefer the students who are dumb jocks (like themselves). Maybe I just didn't like having the tables turned on me since I was usually a teacher's pet in more academic classes.

I also had a terrible time in summer sports day camp. I was supposed to learn to swim but I only got my sinuses full of chlorinated water. There was an even wider range of baffling sports in which I had no better skill than I had exhibited during the school year... it turned out I was also terrible at tennis and golf.

By the time I got to college, I realized that there was a way to take back the control that I'd been missing. I could fulfill the Physical Education requirements by taking modern dance classes. I enjoyed participating, felt more comfortable with my body, was doing something with an artistic component, and ended up taking even more classes than the minimum requirement.

I also had some fun in college playing soccer on an intramural team with friends who didn't take the whole thing too seriously. One of my friends named the team the Slut Puppies. We were consistently among the worst in the league. The other physical activities I've enjoyed have been primarily non-team-oriented. I like bike riding (but not bike maintenance). When I used to live in a place with snow I would go cross-country skiing. Going hiking with friends is a nice way to combine physical and social activity.

Recently there's been a group of people in San Francisco organizing a monthly queer and genderfuck playground, where people play volleyball, basketball, wrestle, and picnic while a DJ plays in a park. Klutzes are encouraged and it's a sort of therapy for people with sports trauma.

For the most part, I hate participating in team sports. I also hate watching sports. My parents were not sports watchers themselves, and I have followed their example. People identify with sports teams that are owned by millionaires. The team members don't even live in the same city as the fans. Residents of the so-called hometown will have riots whether the team wins or loses. The economic benefit to the city of having a sports team is unproven. It's like the modern version of bread and circuses.

Out there in America there are people who are filling their heads with the trivia from the backs of baseball cards and throwing away the gum. At least my music trivia can benefit me as a musician. Sports trivia is only good for making small-talk with other sports maniacs and alienating people who don't like sports.

Nerd Culture: An Appreciation

"Nerd Culture" seems like a contraction in terms. Nerds are supposed to be uncultured but they are not dumb, just lacking in social graces. They have their own culture. Nerds are enthusiastic. If you've ever been cornered by a pair of *Monty Python's Flying Circus* fans recounting a favorite routine, you know that enthusiasm. Breathless words spilling out in nasal inflection, short barking eccentric laughs, eyes manic. Talking to a "normal," the nerd's nature may be hidden. But lo, if that shared computer interest or fandom commonality is revealed, they flip into another mode.

Sometime visit a place where a group of people are playing Dungeons and Dragons or some such fantasy game. The participants gleefully describe the actions of their characters, cleverly outwitting the Dungeon Master, only to be overcome by even more sophisticated traps. A roll of the dice dishes out damage. Disputes arise when a player chooses actions antithetical to the randomly determined traits of the character he controls.

Nerds are largely male, although there are a few females. I have no more explanation for this than for gender representation in other youth subcultures, such as punks, hip-hop fans, etc. Many nerds seem asexual; it's hard to imagine people who have a fixation in childhood pursuits and an immature worldview being anything but virgins.

Nerd music is generally anything you could hear on *The Dr. Demento Show*. The common trait is humor, goofiness. Nerds are not concerned if this is cool or hip. The prime example is Weird Al Yankovic. I've heard They Might Be Giants on the show and while they may be nerd-damage, hiply parodying the geek look, the goofiness of their songs includes them in the genre. Devo is classic nerd culture. Nerds with no concept of hip music will know and love Devo. (No disrespect to Devo intended.) The sophisticated nerd might even listen to The Residents or Captain Beefheart.

In terms of music creation, "filking" is a word applied to songs, generally folkish in nature with lyrical content related to fantasy or science fiction. Nerds are never afraid of being too twee. For example, The Society for Creative Anachronism is a group that dresses up in costumes of several hundred years ago, and has get-togethers where they speak in Elizabethan English. The same people are often involved in Renaissance Feastivals, where they "entertain" guests shopping for candles and pottery with tableaux of sword-fighting and debauchery. Juggling is a skill a few dexterous nerds practice, and they may also be found at such Faires.

The Adventures of Buckaroo Banzai Across the 8th Dimension is the ultimate nerd movie. With the cultishness of a *Rocky Horror Picture Show* groupie (but without the makeup), a nerd will be able to recite all the good lines and says, "Wherever you go, there you are," at least weekly. *Monty Python* is another nerd culture classic. *Revenge of the Nerds*, while cast as nerd parody, is generally liked by nerds. Actually, not all of the so-called nerds in the film are nerds per se but are generally misfits, including a druggie, a musical prodigy, and a homosexual. There's also an accordion-playing female nerd.

Star Trek is a perpetual nerd favorite. Along with comics, science fiction books, and computers, there are nerd cultural festivals, known as Cons, devoted to *Star Trek*. These arefrequently named after the locale, such as the Minneapolis-based MinCon.

Among computer nerds, the main activity is using computers. They stare fixedly at video screens, talk to themselves, occasionally laugh out loud at some insight, then furiously type faster with four fingers than most touch-typists can with ten. I should know because it's into this category that I most squarely fall, although I also like science fiction, comics, and *Star Trek*.

Computer nerds have food needs related to computing. Food should require minimal time away from the computer to obtain, and be possible to eat while hacking. Pizza delivery and vending machine foods like Cheetos, chips, and candy satisfy these conditions. One wants to stay awake and alert so products with maximum sugar and caffeine such as Jolt Cola and Mountain Dew are beverages of choice.

In the 1940s, the late physicist Richard Feynman worked on the Manhattan Project developing the first atomic bomb. He practiced safecracking as a hobby. His book, *Surely You're Joking, Mr. Feynman*, is a nerd classic. Other nerd role models include Steve Wozniak, co-founder of Apple Computer, and John Draper AKA Captain Crunch, famed phone phreaker. (A phreaker is to telephones as a hacker is to computers. Draper's moniker came from his discovery of a cereal-box whistle that emitted a phone-accessing tone.)

Oddly, there is now Nerd Chic. At the dawn of the Internet, there was a hip nerd magazine, *Mondo 2000*. "Smart drinks" replaced Jolt Cola as the beverage of choice (although caffeine was an ingredient in some of the advertised pep-up concoctions, buffered by more arcane chemicals). Buzzwords like "Cyberpunk" and "Virtual Reality" abounded. Folks who started with Dungeons and Dragons began experimenting with the S&M kind of dungeon.

* * *

A Day in the Life of a Nerd

I get up in the morning, trip over the juggling balls I dropped last night, and knock down a pile of science fiction novels piled beside the futon. I shower but don't use deodorant. I brush my hair and put on my glasses. I go outside to wait for my ride to work. I'm a computer programmer. In the car, we talk about a British comedy TV show. Tom has been soldering together a Nintendo PowerGlove for a do-it-yourself virtual reality system. At work, I have a dome in which I'm growing mushrooms. After work, I go to a comic shop. I buy some comics, then get home in time to catch *Star Trek*. I order a pizza. I log in to a computer bulletin board. People are chatting about meeting face-to-face at a science fiction convention. Finally, it's time for sleep, so I put on my pajamas and get into bed.

Medium Media

My parents did not own a television in 1966 when I was born. They got one around 1970 when the elder of my two younger brothers was born. It was a black and white TV and I'm told that I insisted that Big Bird was yellow on the television, probably based on the photo of the giant bird costume with members of the show's cast in *Life* magazine.

That black and white TV was replaced several years later by a color television in a mock-colonial style with a matching pedestal. On that television I watched *The Electric Company*, *Land of the Lost*, *CBS Evening News with Walter Cronkite*, *All In The Family*, *Good Times*, *Planet of the Apes*, the *Six Million Dollar Man*, *H.R. Pufnstuf*, and *Roots*.

I did not watch any television shows except those selected by my parents in the evenings. In the afternoons I would occasionally watch game shows, especially if there were babysitters. I saw a few Marx Brothers movies in afternoons as well. The television would never be on during dinnertime. We'd listen to the radio during breakfast though.

I did not listen to commercial radio. We only listened to public radio: classical music, news programs, and *A Prairie Home Companion*. I also listened to public radio productions of *A Hitchhiker's Guide to the Galaxy* and *Star Wars*. I mostly liked science fiction and fantasy movies, such as *Lord of the Rings*, *Watership Down*, and *Raiders of the Lost Ark*. I would see some movies my parents wanted to watch, like *Kramer vs. Kramer* and *On Golden Pond*.

The toys I had were teddy bears, Tinkertoys, Fisher-Price Little People playsets, Lincoln Logs, Lego, and other creative toys. My brother had a *Six Million Dollar Man* doll. No G.I. Joes.

I read constantly. Mostly fantasy and science fiction, starting with juvenile material and continuing to adult pulp.

Once I reached college I got into punk music, listening to what my friends liked first and then striking out on my own. I went to college film society movies sometimes but only if friends recommended them highly. I didn't own a television in college, though I would sometimes watch in dorm lounges with friends: David Letterman, *the Prisoner*, and even *the Cosby Show*. Perhaps this all has something to do with why I am not now in thrall to mainstream entertainment. I don't watch TV unless someone makes me. Likewise, I feel no compulsion to go to Hollywood movies.

My mother decried bar-going as "passive entertainment." I don't drink, smoke, or do drugs. My biggest compulsion is computer use. I first used a computer in 5th grade, and even before that I can remember visiting college computer rooms where my parents fed decks of punchcards into giant machines. I started getting paid for computer programming the summer after 9th grade and bought my first computer, an Apple II Plus, around that time. My mother would sometimes hide the power cord to keep me from using it too much after school. I still spend several hours a day in front of a computer even when I'm not getting paid to do so.

I didn't have a computer in my dorm room at college. There was a gap of a couple years after college where I didn't have a computer at home and would just use one when I went to Kinko's to rent out time or at a college computer lab.

I didn't have a television at home until I moved in with Nick, the first partner I ever lived with. He had a small black and white TV initially, but eventually bought a small used color TV and a VCR from a relative. At times when I've been a car-bound commuter I've listened to a lot of radio, but I don't much anymore. Generally when I do, it's NPR or local college stations. Usually there are no commercial stations programmed on the radio presets. I read newspapers constantly though I don't subscribe to daily papers. I usually read them in a coffeeshop as other people's discards or online. I always read the free weeklies, the gay papers and, sometimes, local ethnic media. I don't buy many magazines but I browse through them at newsstands.

I was not fed much junk food as a kid (though it was not so forbidden as to turn me into a reactionary), which has led to me being an adult health food nut. I have to guess that the fact that my media consumption was similarly balanced in childhood has led me to the moderate media habits I have as a grown-up.

The Curse of Ham

By and large, I don't pay a whole lot of attention to the pronouncements written in the Bible. By the time I'm done with lunch I've probably violated half a dozen commandments on subjects such as the wearing of mixed fibers, lying with a man as with a woman, and so forth (only being a vegetarian keeps me accidentally kosher). But there's one Biblical injunction that I'm firmly in agreement with and that's the prohibition on seeing one's parents nude.

Most people are familiar with the story of Noah. It's in the book of Genesis, the first part of the Old Testament, if you want to look it up. You know: ark, animals, flood, and so on. Most people, if asked to recount the story, would end when the ark touches down and everyone piles out and lives happily ever after.

But at the risk of anticlimax, there's more. Noah plants a vineyard and makes wine. He gets so trashed that he passes out naked in his tent. His son Ham wanders in and sees his father naked. The other two sons drape a cloth over their shoulders and walk backwards into Noah's tent, covering him up without actually beholding his nakedness. Unfortunately for Ham, his descendents are cursed forever, providing fodder for racists who use this as justification for their bigotry.

So, in other words, you aren't supposed to see your parents naked or you'll have a curse placed on you and all your descendents. While I'm not likely to have any descendents, and I don't really place a whole lot of faith in curses, I'd just as soon not face the sight of my parents nude. I know of no New Testament pronouncement that overrides this prohibition, though my knowledge of the Bible is minimal.

I have to admit that I have seen my parents nude in the past. I'm a child of the '60s, and my parents were liberal and didn't believe in body shame and all that. They typically slept in the nude. So from the time I was young, I did see my parents nude. Besides around bedtime, that would also happen when putting on swimsuits. There were also the times in Norway when I was 10 years old and would share the shower and sit in the sauna with my father at the public baths.

It has fortunately been some time since I have seen my parents nude. However, recently they purchased some land by a lake in northern Minnesota and had a sauna built. The log cabin with the sauna room is charming, and I love sleeping in it when I visit them. But there are always dark hints of firing up the sauna, heating it to a steamy heat somewhere above the body's natural temperature, and all of us—my father, my mother, and I—cramming in there.

A more rational fear might be burning some exposed body part on the red-hot sauna stove (fortunately electrocution from pouring water on an electric sauna stove is not a possibility with a wood-fired oven). What I truly fear is the possibility of being nude in that small space with my parents.

So far we have ended up wiling away the evenings eating, reading, or watching movies, and everyone has gotten too tired to make our way across the snowy yard from the main house out to the sauna. But I dread that someday the inevitable will arrive.

It's not simple ageism—my parents are fairly physically fit, with their summer bike riding and winter skiing. It's a fear of being naked in front of them as well as a fear of them being naked in front of me. I'm still basically a repressed American Protestant and my parents seem to have forgotten that they are, too. There's not a drop of Scandinavian blood in our veins even if some of my mother's in-laws are Nordic. It's these relatives' uninhibited nude rolling in the snow that set the bad example my parents are following. These Northerners, who retain more than a vestige of their pagan origins (though they are church-going, by the way), seem content to ignore this God-given commandment even if they follow many others strictures of the scriptures which I do not.

I have on my own fired up the sauna and sweated in solitude, pouring water from a wooden bucket onto the rocks from whence a cloud of steam rises, warming my body and causing the needle on the wall thermometer to move. I likewise pour cold water on my head and body, convulsing with the shock, but soon enough I am reheated by the stove's emanations. I enjoyed this pleasure in a solitary fashion but I did not discuss it with my parents. It seemed that it might be too much of an encouragement and reminder of something that I do not wish to do.

Bullies

Bullying is picking on someone who cannot defend themselves. And it's not just doing that once, it's a repeated pattern of choosing as victims easy targets who are unable to fight back effectively. I was physically bullied as a child. Stronger boys with muscles would thwack me in the back of the head as I sat in band class or walked down the hall. Guys would steal my hats and mittens. I was taunted for my weakness. Who knows whether these guys had some insight into the future that I myself lacked when they called me a "fag" or whether they simply used the term as a general synonym for "wimp"?

I didn't tell my parents or teachers about these incidents. Maybe adults could have offered more effective means of dealing with the situation if we had discussed it. Fortunately, my stint as punching bag was not too extreme or unending. My belief is that many of those bullies have today achieved less in life than I have. I imagine that they are now mostly unemployed, aging, and unloved (but hopefully not still abusing people around them).

There is a theory that bullies were once picked on themselves by more powerful people and that is why they are now visiting similar abuse on the weak. For instance, bullies may have been abused by adults. My fighting with my younger brother may have been in part in reaction to the bullying I was subjected to outside of my home. He's more than three years younger than me, and I was able to physically dominate him, though not without a struggle. We wrestled, never fighting with fists. I would let him win from time to time, especially if he got really upset while fighting. There were times I even had to let him sit on my head.

I wonder if my past history of being bullied has led me to be another sort of bully as an adult. Not physically—I have not exchanged blows or wrestled with someone since high school—but rather, have I become a mental bully, lording my knowledge and education over those who have weaker learning? There's no pride to be found in winning arguments with people unequipped to defend themselves, who are sometimes so outstripped that they can't even recognize their loss.

For instance, while attending a suburban rally to protest an appearance by George W. Bush, I and other protestors confronted flag-waving Bush loyalists. At a certain point, the Bush-ites resorted to the classic bully-victim tactic of simply ignoring us left-wing bullies and pretending we weren't there hectoring them about their lack of knowledge of U.S. government wrong-doing. Our actions didn't do much to change their minds but made us as bullies feel self-righteous about being more informed than these sheep-like followers.

I also fantasize about physically abusing those whom I dislike. Examples of people I have such fantasies about include government officials whose actions have resulted in large numbers of civilian deaths, bank scandal criminals who have increased the public debt, and other unpunished perpetrators of injustice. If such action by someone upsets me, I sometimes have fantasies of hitting them in the kneecaps with a bat, making them suffer as they have made others suffer. But it doesn't seem logical, I would never actually carry out such a plan. I'm opposed to capital punishment and other prison system cruelty. What person is going to change because someone physically assaults them? My rage should be channeled into other forms of expression.

Bullying is a form of domesticated terrorism, keeping the victim in a state of compliance through continually enforced fear. Herding them into doing what you want. But the bully does not really know what he wants: he's not in control, he's controlled by psychological programming that he has received. What does the bully really want? He wants to feel powerful and strong. By having control over others, he regains the power that he lost.

Sick Days

When I was a kid, I'd get sick and stay home by myself. I'd make Jell-O and lie on the couch, sleeping fitfully, sweating, and watching TV. I might put on some records. Once when I had the flu I listened to Black Sabbath's first album which my parents inexplicably owned. Its woozy atmosphere matched my symptoms.

I've spent the last week sick. I didn't puke or anything, but I felt low on energy, sweaty, and didn't feel like doing much. I interpreted it as flu. It didn't seem like a cold. I never took my temperature but there were probably some mild fevers. Nothing like SARS or H1N1. What do people do who have chronic illness? Would my bad day seem like a good day to them? Would they be able to work through what I find debilitating? Am I being a wimp? On the other hand, maybe it's good that I slept a lot and didn't stress myself out. It might have made me get better faster.

I guess I could have let my partner have the bed and gone to sleep in the living room... quarantined myself to avoid spreading germs. I did that by not going out much but I missed the social aspect of city living, being able to get out of the house, doing stuff, meeting people.

One night I went out to see a film at the Red Vic movie house on Haight Street. I ran into a few people I knew. I looked unshaven and messy-haired, and felt like I'd shuffled out of the house in a robe and slippers. I told them I was sick and kept my distance.

I'm still coughing. I still have yellow mucus. I still have a sinus infection, I'm pretty sure. I avoid antibiotics. It's not worth it to mess up my digestion. I also don't have proper health insurance. This illness will pass but I worry that it will spread to a lung condition like pneumonia or that I'll get an ear infection. Are there long-term effects of this illness? Does it weaken or strengthen an immune system? I guess if there's a lung problem then there can be scarring from that. Is the coughing popping my alveoli and leading to reduced lung capacity?

I don't know how I got sick. Who had the same symptoms I do? I have been around some people like Checkers with his throat clearing, but this doesn't seem like quite the same thing. Am I still contagious? Does my partner have the same thing I did, since his symptoms don't seem to be the same as mine? This is just something I go through once a year or so. I haven't had a real flu with throwing up and so on for quite a while though I get the sinus infections pretty often. Is it the mold in the apartment or an allergy to cats? Should I get some sort of decongestant?

Someone is sure to tell me about some sort of folk remedy involving garlic or some sort of thing that's supposed to act as nature's antibiotic. Side effects of bad breath are probably better than ruining the stomach fauna. Speaking of which, I should really get some acidophilus. There are the times that I can breathe clearly through both nostrils, and I tell myself that I'm finally over it, I'm going to be fine from here on out. Pretty soon it comes back and I'm congested again. It's chronic.

I read up on what could be prescribed. There is some sort of drug that disrupts the viral process, some sort of enzyme inhibitor, but even if it's prescribed right away, it only shortens the duration of the illness by a day or so. It does reduce contagion as well, though, so I suppose that result is worthwhile. If there were some major outbreak of killer flu, I hope they have some reserves of that drug built up.

Why does it have to happen to me? Why can't I have some sort of super-immunity? Never get sick. Never have to waste time blowing my nose and napping. It's a mild illness, and it will pass and be forgotten like every past one.

Sperm Donation

An unusual email arrived the other day. A woman wrote to say that a friend of hers was considering having a child, and they were wondering if I would be willing to donate sperm. The idea was not to prompt a co-parenting situation, just a donation of some raw materials. I'm flattered that someone would want my semen. They must think my mental and physical traits are desirable (though certain lesbians consider David Crosby an ideal sperm donor).

After reflecting on the request a bit, I was inclined to decline. I don't understand caving in to the impulse to have biological children. Here's a parallel in the animal kingdom: my cats are neutered because it's irresponsible to bring more kittens into the world when there are so many homeless cats in pounds and running around feral. And the impact of a cat on the planet is so much less than the impact of a human. There are plenty of neglected children out there needing foster-care and adoption.

Some people feel that their cat or dog is something really special and they think its offspring would be better than the average unadopted animal in the pound. That just doesn't make sense. The whole phenomenon of purebred dogs and cats is ridiculous. Some people want to have a child who is biologically their own rather than adopting. I don't see much of a difference.

Consider this: who do you like better, your relatives or your friends? Someone's biological relationship to you is no guarantee that they're going to be someone you get along with or agree with. My brother has gotten a vasectomy, and his wife is into the child-free movement. Even the supposed breeders in my family aren't going to breed. I shouldn't add to the irony by becoming a sperm donor.

I'm not against people being parents. I know more people

with biological children than adopted ones. I assume many of the heterosexuals I know who have kids were simply sloppy with their birth control method, since we all know how sexually irresponsible straights are.

So much for my annoying judgments on other people: how would I measure up as a parental figure? I couldn't give enough of my time to being a full-time parent. I like kids okay (though I feel uncomfortable with acting as an authority figure and would rather act like a big kid and play). I'm more comfortable being a mentor to older youth who have already had a chance to develop their own personalities and influence but still have enthusiasm for learning. Parenting a kid might be a great learning experience and lead to learning how to accomplish other things in life more efficiently... but it's not going to happen.

VIII. Wants vs. Needs

I Want to Interrogate America

I want answers to my questions. I'm tired of being ignored. I want some responses. I want to know how people in this country can be brainwashed so effectively. I want to know how they can put their trust in the hands of people whose interests are in opposition to their own. I want to know how people have been trained to misdirect their rage against people who are as oppressed or more oppressed than they are, rather than fighting those who are oppressing all. I want to ask the right questions to make people realize that their preconceptions are incorrect. I want to walk down every road in America and speak to every child and adult. I want to see a spark of recognition in people's eyes, for them to realize that someone is speaking their language. I want to find the reason corporations are allowed to exist and destroy. I want to find out why people don't know history. I want to learn along with America. I want to teach America how to read, write, and speak. I want to have a dialog with America. I want to get America to stop shouting and have a conversation. I want America to take the flag down for a day. I want America to visit other countries. I want America to admit that this is not the best of all possible worlds. I want America to acknowledge its mistakes. I want America to follow some better examples. I want America to explain what's the theory behind its practice.

I want America to gain consciousness.

Leave Me Alone

Please leave me alone. I need some time to concentrate on my own stuff. Please give me some space to think. There is not enough room or time here. I need to relax. I need to listen to music. I need to be able to control my own space. I need to have time. I need to take a long walk in the park. I need to breathe deeply. I need a long hot bath. I need to stay in the shower longer. I need to masturbate. I need to lie naked in the sun. I need to be away from the sound of an internal combustion engine. I need to drive a long time. I need to choose my own adventure. I need to listen on headphones. I need to get into my own trip.

If I smoked pot I would need to smoke it now. If I drank alcohol I would need a cold drink now. If I meditated I would need to meditate now. I don't have these things so I need some time and space and freedom and silence and control. So please leave me alone, go find your own space, go listen to your own music somewhere else because I need this afternoon (this evening, this night, this space) free.

I need to rent a hotel room so I can get some decent sleep. I need to go sleep in a tent under the stars since I can't see the stars here due to the city lights. I need to go somewhere very quiet for a while so I can continue to take the things that have to happen—that I have to go through for living—to continue... but what's the point of going on when I never get any peace and quiet?

Now it's peaceful, now it's quiet. Now I need to hold that thought. Hold that thought for a little while until I'm completely calm and cool and collected. Random thoughts need to float free and leave me at peace.

Neoconservative

Stop the presses. I've decided to become a Neoconservative. I am leaving the Left behind and joining the Right Wing. I'm ready to lick the hand of the corporate masters. I'm ready to embrace Republicanism. I'm ready to learn to stop repudiating my bigotry and turn it into a virtue. I'm going to attack and rat out everyone who used to be my ally. Nobody will ever trust me again, neither the radicals nor the conservatives. I'm cutting the rope to the anchor. Nobody will ever know in which direction my boat sails again. People will wonder if I'm doing it for the money or was just driven crazy from the frustration. I'm giving up my wavering between democracy and anarchism, and embracing fascism. Might makes right. Why lend my weak force to the opposition when I can join the powerful majority? Power is attractive. I'm tired of resisting. Now I know how Darth Vader felt.

I used to have ideals. I used to have core values. I used to side with the underdog. I used to want to overthrow the unjustly powerful.

I used to want to create change. I used to want to empower the weak. I used to want to not benefit from privilege. I used to want to help people learn. I used to want to encourage creativity. I used to be tolerant. I used to be solicitous.

But I've been worn down by the world. I've learned to blame the poor, blame the oppressed. I hold innocent the rich, the powerful, the entitled. What I used to think were symptoms, I now believe to be instigators. What I used to believe were causes of suffering, I now believe are saviors. I'm like one of those optical illusions that has flipped from appearing convex to appearing concave. All my beliefs have turned themselves inside out.

My old allies will always call me a turncoat; those I now try to appease will brand me untrustworthy. Too many like me before have shifted course once, then again. Too many people have attacked and defended, then attacked again. There is no reason to put trust in inconsistency.

I may have no evidence but I attack others for having no evidence. I nitpick but don't worry about my side's inaccuracy. I publish no corrections. Vitriol pays my bills. I am an actor who can only portray the emotion of anger. I am the new editor of the Delta Mirror in this brave new world. I am a cynic who kicks dogs.

Behind my back they say I'm bitter. They say I don't really believe what I'm saying now. They dig out things I wrote twenty years ago to show that I can't really believe what I'm saying. But people change. They say I'm wrong now but I say I was wrong then. Before I was a moral relativist but now I am following natural law and Biblical values. How are my statements any less true than those of someone who has been a conservative all along? I've seen the light, had a conversion on the road. They're just afraid that the same thing is going to happen to them. That one day they'll see that liberalism is just internalized guilt, that there is no shame in promoting business that will lead to economic wellbeing for this great nation.

The true oppressors in our society are not the people who are running businesses and making money from the stock market. The true oppressors are those who try to stifle conservatives on campus through claims of racism and sexism. Feminism has resulted in a world that is worse for women as well as men. Affirmative action is unnecessary and leads to rewarding people who are less qualified. The gay rights movement is being hijacked by the Left Wing. Marxism has led to great suffering around the world. We can bring democracy to countries by using our military technology. We can stimulate the economy through giving tax cuts to the wealthy.

Now that I have these views, I find it much easier to get paid for having my words published. Editors are beating down my doors to write opinion pieces. I have started appearing on television as a commentator. This never happened before I became a Neoconservative. I am happy to finally be justly rewarded.

I pledge allegiance to the mighty power of the grand conservative traditional values of these United States of America.

Reasons to Live

I know I complain a lot. My formula is to figure out something that annoys me and go on about that at length. For a change, I'm going to accentuate the positive. Look on the bright side… all those clichés. Cynicism, stay at bay for a minute. I'm looking for my silver lining. Maybe it's still at the drycleaners.

A cat purring on your lap. Fresh bread. The transcendence offered by the best music. An orgasm, whether self-administered or with the help of a friend. Walking in the rain by choice. The pleasure of having created. The elation of a successful performance. The joy of love reciprocated. A deep massage. The excitement of finding a long sought collectable. Seeing films projected in a movie palace. Chocolate cake. Good conversation with an understanding friend. A deep massage. Coltrane. Cuddling. Richard Strauss. These are a few of my favorite things.

Yet it is more satisfying to complain about what is wrong than to try to praise that which is right. How can we make the world a place where more people can experience life's pleasures more often? Why can't every meal be transcendent, every interpersonal interaction enjoyable? Are these peak experiences so good only because they are so often separated not merely by valleys but ravines of bad times?

About the Author

Larry-bob Roberts is into sparking culture, politics, and creating fusions between the two. Cultural activism, independent music, spoken word performance, and event production, as well as involvement in electoral politics are the areas in which he operates.

Since 1989, he has been publishing in print and now online the zine, *Holy Titclamps* (www.holytitclamps.com). He currently plays piano in The Winsome Griffles, and maintains a local weekly queer cultural calendar, *Queer Things To Do* (SFQueer.com), as well as the QComedy.com website. Roberts co-hosts a long-running monthly spoken word, music, comedy, and performance open mic, "Smack Dab" at Magnet. He currently resides in San Francisco with his partner, Tommy Netzband.